BRIGHT NOTES

THE MAJOR PLAYS OF EUGENE O'NEILL

Intelligent Education

Nashville, Tennessee

BRIGHT NOTES: The Major Plays of Eugene O'Neill
www.BrightNotes.com

No part of this publication may be used or reproduced in any manner whatsoever without written permission, except in the case of brief quotations in critical articles and reviews. For permissions, contact Influence Publishers http://www.influencepublishers.com.

ISBN: 978-1-645424-44-4 (Paperback)
ISBN: 978-1-645424-45-1 (eBook)

Published in accordance with the U.S. Copyright Office Orphan Works and Mass Digitization report of the register of copyrights, June 2015.

Originally published by Monarch Press.
David Madison Rogers, 1965
2020 Edition published by Influence Publishers.

Interior design by Lapiz Digital Services. Cover Design by Thinkpen Designs.

Printed in the United States of America.

Library of Congress Cataloging-in-Publication Data forthcoming.
Names: Intelligent Education
Title: BRIGHT NOTES: The Major Plays of Eugene O'Neill
Subject: STU004000 STUDY AIDS / Book Notes

CONTENTS

1)	Introduction to Eugene O'Neill	1
2)	Introduction to Anna Christie	7
3)	Anna Christie: Character Analysis	9
4)	Anna Christie: Summary	12
5)	Anna Christie: Essay Questions and Answers	15
6)	Introduction to The Emperor Jones	17
7)	The Emperor Jones: Character Analysis	23
8)	The Emperor Jones: Essay Questions and Answers	27
9)	Introduction to The Hairy Ape	29
10)	The Hairy Ape: Character Analysis	35
11)	The Hairy Ape: Essay Questions and Answers	39
12)	Introduction to Desire Under the Elms	41

13)	Desire Under the Elms: Character Analysis	43
14)	Desire Under the Elms: Essay Questions and Answers	48
15)	Introduction to Strange Interlude	50
16)	Strange Interlude: Character Analysis	52
17)	Strange Interlude: Essay Questions and Answers	59
18)	Introduction to Mourning Becomes Electra	61
19)	Mourning Becomes Electra: Character Analysis	64
20)	Mourning Becomes Electra: Essay Questions and Answers	75
21)	Introduction to Ah, Wilderness!	77
22)	Ah, Wilderness!: Character Analysis	79
23)	Ah, Wilderness!: Summary	82
24)	Ah, Wilderness!: Essay Questions and Answers	85
25)	Introduction to The Iceman Cometh	87
26)	The Iceman Cometh: Character Analysis	89
27)	The Iceman Cometh: Summary	92
28)	The Iceman Cometh: Essay Questions and Answers	95
29)	Introduction to Long Day's Journey Into Night	97

30)	Long Day's Journey Into Night: Character Analysis	99
31)	Long Day's Journey Into Night: Essay Questions and Answers	105
32)	Introduction to A Touch of the Poet	107
33)	A Touch of the Poet: Character Analysis	109
34)	A Touch of the Poet: Summary	111
35)	A Touch of the Poet: Essay Questions and Answers	114
36)	Conclusion	116
37)	Bibliography	120

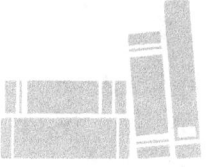

EUGENE O'NEILL

INTRODUCTION

EARLY LIFE

Eugene O'Neill was born in a Broadway hotel on October 16, 1888. His father was a popular actor of romantic melodrama and Eugene's first seven years were spent in the larger towns all over the United States. The success of the *Count of Monte Cristo*, in which his father played the lead, kept the family engaged in almost continuous road tours. From the age of seven to thirteen he attended boarding schools. In 1902 he was sent to Betts Academy at Stamford and the autumn after his graduation he entered Princeton. Although his parents were Catholic, and he had been in and out of parochial schools from an early age, by the time he entered Princeton he had left the Church and never returned to it.

DISCONTENT WITH COLLEGE

In June of 1903 he was dismissed from Princeton, supposedly for throwing a beer bottle through a window of President Wilson's house. He could have returned the following year, but he had become bored with college and left to become a secretary in a New York mail-order house, the first in a long series of jobs he held before settling down to write.

YEARS OF WANDERING

In 1909 he married Kathleen Jenkins, a union that ended in divorce in 1912. In the same year he went on a gold-prospecting trip to Honduras. He had been reading Jack London, Kipling and Conrad, and we can see in the many journeys of his youth a desire to lead the rugged life of adventure that those writers took as their central **theme**. In 1910 he shipped on a Norwegian barque for Buenos Aires where he worked at some odds jobs, but ended up, in his own words, "a bum on the docks." In 1911, after a trip to Africa on a cattle steamer, he returned to New York where he lived at "Jimmy the Priest's," a waterfront dive which provided the setting for the first act of *Anna Christie*. After a last voyage to England he found himself on a train to New Orleans following a wild party. His father was playing there in the perennially popular *Monte Cristo*. He refused to give his son a handout, but did give him a part in the play. At the close of the season the O'Neills returned to their summer home in New London, Connecticut, where Eugene worked as a cub reporter on the *Telegraph*.

HIS DESIRE TO WRITE

In December of 1912 O'Neill entered a tuberculosis sanatorium. Weakened by years of irregular living, his health had broken down. During his fifteen month convalescence he first felt the urge to write. When he left the sanatorium he was a man with a purpose. To rebuild his health he disciplined himself to a life of exercise and hard work. In the next sixteen months he wrote eleven one-act plays, two long plays, and some poetry. He read omnivorously, in his own words "the Greeks and Elizabethans- practically all the classics - and of course all the moderns."

FIRST PLAYS

In the fall of 1914 he went to Harvard to take Professor George Baker's famous course in playwriting. In the same year his father financed the publication of his first book, *Thirst and Other One-act Plays*. Several plays in *Thirst* take men against the sea as their **theme**. O'Neill's classic statement of his **theme** is in the so-called Glencairn group, a sequence of one-act plays dealing with the tramp steamer Glencairn. The group consists of *The Moon of the Caribbees, Bound East for Cardiff, The Long Voyage, Home* and *In the Zone*. In these plays man is shown in conflict with nature, which is indifferent to his suffering and inevitable doom. In his early naturalism O'Neill was deeply indebted to Jack London.

FIRST SUCCESS

In 1916 the Provincetown Players put on *Bound East for Cardiff*. It was O'Neill's first play to be acted. The Players were a group of Greenwich Village journalists, writers and painters who were interested in rejuvenating the American theater. In 1917-18 he had three plays published in *Smart Set*, a magazine of protest against the self-satisfied middle class, whose editors, H. L. Mencken and George Jean Nathan, were already known as literary critics. The production of *Beyond the Horizon* in 1920 brought O'Neill his first Pulitzer Prize, and from then until his death no one seriously questioned that he was the leading

American playwright of his generation. In 1918 he had married Agnes Boulton Burton, and now, riding the wave of success, he had great faith in the future. However, he resolved he would never sell out to success. His father had felt that the temptation of easy money to be had from a play such as *Monte Cristo* had ruined his chances of becoming a fine actor. O'Neill resolved he would remain true to his dream and work to express the truth he had in him.

DISILLUSIONMENT

In spite of his remarkable success, O'Neill was convinced that bad fortune was hounding him. Throughout his life, except for brief periods, he had the feeling that man is at the mercy of mysterious forces beyond his control. He began to look back with nostalgia upon his seafaring days, and longed to be on the move again.

FINANCIAL SUCCESS

In the fall of 1920 *The Emperor Jones* was staged in London, Paris, Berlin, Tokyo and Buenos Aires, laying the foundation for O'Neill's international reputation. One year later *Anna Christie* opened in New York and brought him his second Pulitzer Prize. In 1922 *The Hairy Ape* was a success. It dramatized the idea that man has lost his old harmony with nature and is out of place in the modern, technological world. Late in 1922 O'Neill was making $850 a week in royalties. He bought a farm at Ridgefield, Connecticut, and settled down to live in landed elegance as his father had always desired to do.

HIS PESSIMISM

However, O'Neill could not settle down and two years later he was living in Bermuda and working on the idea for *Mourning Becomes Electra*. His idea of man at the mercy of mysterious forces had broadened through his reading of Freud, a German psychologist (1856-1939), Nietzsche, a German ethical writer who detested Christianity (1844-19000), and Schopenhauer, a German philosopher of the romantic period (1788-1860). From Freud he took the idea of man trapped by his unconscious sexual desires. Schopenhauer's pessimistic philosophy reinforced the naturalistic determinism that had been fostered by his reading of London and Conrad, and his own erratic life. From Nietzsche he took a joyous acceptance of despair as the only sane attitude for a man faced with an indifferent universe.

HONORED FOR HIS WORK

In 1926 he received the degree of Doctor of Literature from Yale University. Although at the height of his career, his personal life was a shambles. The following year he left his wife and two children to court Carlotta Monterey, the actress who had starred in *The Hairy Ape*. In 1928 *Strange Interlude* won a third Pulitzer Prize for him. Eugene and Carlotta took a whirlwind trip around the world and settled in a French chateau where he finished *Mourning Becomes Electra*. The play was presented in New York in October of 1931 and was immediately hailed as his masterpiece. Joseph Wood Krutch wrote that "it may turn out to be the only permanent contribution yet made by the twentieth century to dramatic literature."

AWARDED NOBEL PRIZE

From 1932 to 1936 O'Neill lived on an island off the coast of Georgia. The only successful play he wrote during this period was *Ah, Wilderness!*, the only comedy he ever composed. The play ran for 289 performances and brought O'Neill $75,000. In November of 1936 he moved to Oregon with plans to write a cycle of plays designed to tell the story of the United States from the early 1700s. In the same month he became the first American playwright to receive the Nobel Prize.

HIS LAST WORK

During the latter part of his life only a few O'Neill plays were produced. In 1941 he completed the autobiographical *Long Day's Journey Into Night* which was first staged in 1956, three years after his death. It won his fourth Pulitzer Prize. His vision of life had not changed and the characters are unable to control the dark forces that shape their destinies. *The Iceman Cometh* was staged in 1946. It was an enormous success, but the play is uncompromisingly nihilistic in its philosophy. He suggests that man's urge toward the unattainable is his only justification, but what the unattainable is he can never know. O'Neill died in 1953 at the age of sixty-five. No one doubted that he was the greatest playwright America had produced.

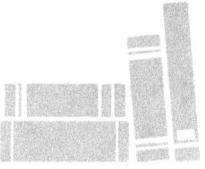

ANNA CHRISTIE

INTRODUCTION

....

Anna Christie was completed in 1920 and produced the following year. O'Neill based it on an older play, Chris Christopherson, about Anna's father. This first version was an imaginative reconstruction of the life and death of a real sailor by the same name. This unfortunate man declared that he hated the sea, as does old Chris in the play. He was found frozen to death after a drunken night at "Jimmy the Priest's," a favorite bar of the young O'Neill. Anna herself was fictional, yet her character came to dominate the play as a whole and ultimately her name became the title of the final version. Perhaps because of the earlier idea for the play, *Anna Christie* tends to fall into two parts, and Anna herself into two characters. The first part is old Chris' reunion with his cynical, fallen daughter and his winning her to the life of the sea in spite of his own fear of that life. The second is Anna's tumultuous love affair with Mat Burke after she has become a "new woman." Critics have indicated that this lack of unity in structure and character is a flaw in an otherwise admirable work.

In *Anna Christie* the characters are initially bound to one another by their weaknesses. Anna seeks out Chris because she is sick and needs rest. Chris wins her confidence because of his simplicity and obvious need for her companionship. Mat first appeals to the man-hating Anna when he shows physical weakness. His attachment to her is based on his need for a pure woman to look up to. He projects his longing for such a woman into Anna. By the end of the play a change has taken place. Anna is strong, healthy, even reborn. Chris has become reconciled to Anna's love for Mat and has signed on for his first real sea voyage in years. Mat has regained his strength and has learned to love a flesh - and blood woman.

O'Neill was annoyed at the suggestion of certain critics that he had given *Anna Christie* a "Hollywood ending." He claimed that he had not meant to indicate either a happy or an unhappy end to the romance of Anna and Mat. The play concludes on the note that the sea directly controls the fate of them all. Anna is to be Mat's wife, and Mat, as well as her father, is to set sail once again. The hint of foreboding does not mean certain doom, merely that all of life (represented by the sea) awaits them. The action of the play is only a brief interlude in their lives and anything may befall them afterwards. Any critical problem about the ending can be resolved by reference to the symbol of the sea in the play.

Men have different relationships with the sea in *Anna Christie*. Old Chris has been the fearful slave of the sea all his life, and for him the sea means suffering, or the working out of man's fate in tragic terms. For Anna, the land was a force for corruption, and the sea means freedom and purification from sin. Mat rises from the sea to meet Anna, and when he wants to marry her, Chris feels that it is really the sea that is taking Anna from him. In loving Mat, with his wild, strong and straightforward attitude toward life, Anna also expresses her love for the sea, which he represents. Anna and Mat meet the sea and their fate with a joyous attitude and with confidence in their freedom. They are not slaves to the sea or to their fate as Chris has always been. For Chris, the sea is the devil, but for Mat, the sea is the will of God.

ANNA CHRISTIE

CHARACTER ANALYSIS

CHRIS CHRISTOPHERSON

Chris is a rough, bulky, squat sailor, about fifty years old. His blue eyes express simple good humor, but his mouth is self-indulgent and weak. He is kind but obstinate. He tends either to boom in conversation or to half-whisper, plaintively. His kindly sentiments are revealed at once by his worry over Marthy's feelings when he must get rid of her. We are shown in advance that Anna will be welcome because of Chris' humane feeling for Marthy. The contrast is puzzling between this spontaneous kindness and the inexcusable lack of care Chris showed for his family. Evidently Chris is capable of expressing love, but not of setting another person above his own self-interest until the very end of the play.

ANNA CHRISTIE

Anna has the tall, blond good looks common to women of her Nordic stock. She is about twenty years old, but already has a harsh, cynical way about her. Even when Anna has become a changed woman, she shows her old rough, impatient manner when she is crossed. At no point does she become soft, feminine or sentimental. Mat, Chris and the audience must learn to accept her as she is, for clearly Anna will not change her basically hard, proud character. Yet despite her toughness, Anna cannot help rising to other people's high opinion of her, even when it is not justified in the light of her past. She avoids ordering hard liquor when Chris wants to buy her a drink, and she is instinctively modest and proper with the devoted Mat Burke.

MARTHY

Anna recognized immediately that Marthy was herself forty years from now, just as Marthy saw that Anna was also a prostitute. There is a strong difference between them, however, that Anna did not perceive. Marthy has been able to enjoy her trade and has a sense of genuine friendship toward her men. Marthy is old, fat, and wheezing, but she has a love for life and a real sympathy for people that is lacking in Anna. Her concern for Chris' relationship with his daughter, even after being thrown off the barge because of Anna, clearly shows Marthy's utter lack of bitterness or selfishness.

MAT BURKE

Mat is a big, tough, defiant stoker of about thirty. It is apparent from the start that he has built himself up in his own eyes as a man of unconquerable strength, endurance and attractiveness to women. His boasting and pride can accomplish nothing, however, against Anna's reserve, suspicion and independence. Mat wants to glorify himself even in his courting of Anna. For the sake of his honor, she must be the purest girl in the world.

His pride in himself was forever shaken by Anna's revelation of her past, and he groans at the thought that a man like him had been "made the fool of the world." In order to marry Anna after knowing the truth about her, Mat must accept a truth about himself also: his need for another person is so great that beside it his honor is nothing.

ANNA CHRISTIE

SUMMARY

ACT I

The first impression we are given in the play is that appearances are deceptive. "Johnny the Priest" has the look of a holy man despite his bad character. This prepares us for the later revelation that Anna is a pure woman despite her heavy make-up and gaudy clothes. We are even more disposed to sympathize with Anna by the information Chris gives us about her childhood. The good character of the jovial Marthy, in spite of her profession, is further evidence that we are not to judge people in the play by the usual moral standards.

The Anna of the first act is almost entirely hard, cynical and lonely. Only Marthy's persevering friendliness is able to penetrate Anna's shell. Still, Anna does not show real warmth at any point in the first act until she has become convinced of Chris' genuine fatherly affection. Her hatred and fear of men is so great that at first she is even suspicious of her father's embrace.

Anna blames her profession on the fact that caring for other people's children made her feel desperately trapped.

Chris blames his weakness as a man on the mysterious sea. Both father and daughter reveal their weaknesses early in the play. It is obvious that Chris uses the sea as a scapegoat, for when he is trying to convince Anna that she should live on the barge, he paints a glowing picture of life at sea. Underneath his fear, he is really attracted by the sea, but he does not admit this except by his final action in the play-signing onto a steamer again.

ACT II

At once we are shown a new Anna, transformed by the life she had always yearned for unconsciously. Before, she had felt caged and dirty. Now she feels purified and released from the grubby life of landsmen. Whenever Chris starts in with his monotonous remarks about the sea's evil, Anna becomes angry. It is as though she senses that he is trying to direct her new life for her as he did in the past with such disastrous results. Initially Anna is repelled by Mart because he is a rough braggart and because he tries to use her as she has been used in the past. Her instincts are now completely those of a decent woman, and we are shown dramatically that her past is really dead.

Mat is quick construct a whole images of Anna based on what he thinks is the real woman. It is not so much Anna herself that he loves, but his idea of her. This is why he proposes so quickly and why it is necessary for him to be shocked by the truth before he can love her as herself. Despite this misunderstanding, Mat and Anna are able to establish a genuine common ground. They both love the sea and find it "clean." When Chris interrupts them angrily and orders Anna to her room, she at once makes it clear to him that she is not his slave.

ACT III

Chris feels the usual aversion of O'Neill heroes for men who run the steamers as opposed to "real" sailors who run clean sailing ships. His basic objection, however, is that of jealousy, like many fathers in O'Neill plays. He tells Burke how Anna is all that is left to him and that he has only had her company a short while. Mat is quick to object that Chris, by his neglect of Anna until recently, has little rightful claim to her devotion. Mat attacks the old man even further, by questioning his manhood, since he has given up the sea out of fear. The physical clash of the two men is the dramatic sign of the emotional conflict between the jealous father and the strong young man. At the very moment the two men are battling over who is to possess her, Anna asserts both her independence and her identity.

ACT IV

Chris wishes he had not been forced to learn Anna's story, and Mat hopes that Anna will tell him it was all a lie. Neither of them can at first accept the real Anna. Chris is quicker to reconcile himself to the truth because he recognizes his responsibility for Anna's condition. The bulk of the fourth act is devoted to the struggles of Mat as he tries to save his love and his honor at the same time. In the end, Mat's love for Anna as she really is strong enough to overcome the unrealistic ideas he had about both life and love. Not only is he able to forgive her past, but unconditionally to forgive the future in advance by his expression of faith in her.

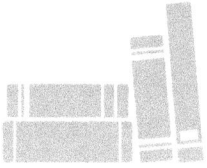

ANNA CHRISTIE

ESSAY QUESTIONS AND ANSWERS

Question: How are the lives of the three main characters affected by the sea? What does the sea represent to them?

Answer: For Anna, the sea is her past and her future. In the past, her father was so dominated by the sea that he left her among strangers. Anna's future marriage to Mat Burke will be dominated by the sea also. We know that he has had a past full of violence and affairs with waterfront women, and we also know his brutal temper. In entrusting herself to Mat as his wife, Anna is running the same sort of risk that the two men run by shipping out for Africa.

The sea intoxicates men with its freedom from responsibility. It causes them to forget their personal obligations. Anna herself rejoices in the feeling of freedom the sea gives her. This freedom is dangerous, for it means that those left at home will suffer like Anna's mother suffered. The sea is life itself, or fate, in the play. As such, it cannot be avoided or fought directly; it can only be endured. The highest degree of virtue in the play is the joyful and fearless acceptance of the sea and all it stands for.

Question: How does Anna's character remain essentially the same throughout the play? In what ways does it change?

Answer: From the beginning of the play, Anna is bitter, unyielding and fiercely independent. She is dominated by hate in the first act, and slowly comes to be dominated by love by the end of the play. Her new freedom on the barge with her father is chiefly responsible for the changes in her attitude. However, she uses the same harsh language throughout the play, and continues to manifest sharp suspicion toward anyone who tries to limit her freedom in any way. Her love for Mat and affectionate tolerance of Chris do not fundamentally alter her vision of life as a lonely, sorrowful business in which men will generally short-change you if they can. Anna's most constant emotions are her hatred of being owned and her love for the sea with the freedom it represents. She is not at all cast down at the thought of being alone in her little house, while the two men are at sea. Now she does not mind being lonely, as long as she is free. All her life, other people have represented only suffering and slavery for Anna.

Any of the changes which occur in Anna's character can be attributed to the love that her two men of the sea are able to draw from her. Anna seems only to love a man when she sees weakness first. Otherwise, the man in his strength is too much of a threat to her independence. Her awareness of the moral weakness of old Chris and the physical weakness of the newly shipwrecked Mat Burke made it possible for Anna to feel compassion. Anna saw Mat's boasting at once for what it was-a weakness like his physical weakness. Anna's new freedom and security gained through life on the barge made her able to feel and express compassion and finally to promise herself to a man out of love.

THE EMPEROR JONES

INTRODUCTION

With the production of *The Emperor Jones* in 1920, Eugene O'Neill's reputation was established. In this play, he had given audiences a new kind of theater experience. Though the staging was unorthodox and thus confusing, the play had power and directness of impact due to its simple structure and elemental **theme**. Essentially, *The Emperor Jones* is a **dramatic monologue**. All the action after the introductory scene occurs at one time and place: in and around the Great Forest, between twilight and dawn. The instinct that drives the main character, a hunted Negro, is the will to power, or pride. This **theme** of the soul in bondage to itself is common in O'Neill's plays. The vice of pride is not recognized by its possessor. It closes him in on all sides, isolating him from others. In this play, pride ends by reducing the hero to the opposite of itself. Jones becomes a pitiful, whimpering bundle of abject superstition at the end of his jungle ordeal.

The production of this play was a beacon of hope for the American theater, which had long been stagnating under the influence of an uninspired **realism** borrowed from Europe. O'Neill overcame the old tradition in a burst of fantasy and symbolism. Yet an almost classical discipline and order dominates the play, and the principle of this order is the philosophy of determinism. The hero is at the mercy of both inward drives and outward circumstances, and his will cannot be considered free in any sense. Jones struggles against his fate throughout the play, but he cannot escape the past of his race and himself.

The belief in determinism was commonplace in the late nineteenth century and the beginning of the twentieth. O'Neill gave artistic expression to the current ideas of his time of the psychology of the will and on evolution. In *The Emperor Jones*, instinct overcomes reason and freedom of the will, and man regresses to his original primitive condition. Instinct is largely a product of the forces of the past at work upon the human mind. The great modern psychologist C. G. Jung believed that the mind is unconsciously aware of many elements that have formed man's past, and he called this accumulation of data the "collective unconscious." O'Neill used this idea fruitfully in *The Emperor Jones*, dramatizing it by the regression of a civilized Negro to the depths of his African past.

The natives of the island have put up with their imported tyrant long enough. While the Emperor, an American named Brutus Jones, takes his customary mid-day nap, they all flee to the hills. Only one old woman remained to be caught on her way from the palace by Smithers, the henchman of the Emperor. Smithers had taken up Jones when he had first arrived in the West Indies, hoping to use him as an instrument to bleed the natives. Jones, however, was too much for him, and took over the island and its goods as his own to plunder. Smithers was allowed only the crumbs from the imperial table, while Jones amassed a private fortune in a foreign bank. Both men regarded the natives with contempt, and thought little of their capacity to retaliate. The story wrung by Smithers from the old woman he had caught sneaking away convinced him that the game was up. His envy and fear of Jones makes his reaction to the news one of spiteful glee.

The Emperor appears in his courtroom earlier than expected, having been wakened by Smither's noise. His shrewdness, physical strength and self-reliance are at once apparent. These qualities are far more integrally a part of him than the absurd grandeur of his comic opera uniform, and Smithers cringes despite his smugness over the news he has to deliver. The two exchange a few taunts about the thefts and prison stretches of their respective pasts before they get down to the business at hand. Jones boasts of his god-like status among the natives since their assassination plot against him failed. He had convinced them that only a silver bullet could kill him and that he himself would be the one it put it in his head. He even shows Smithers a silver bullet he had made and which he keeps as a sort of charm against disaster.

When it is clear to Jones that the natives have run off for good, he wastes no time in regret over his lost empire, but walks proudly out the main door. His plan, which he confides to Smithers, is to strike out through the jungle on a path he knows well and where he has buried canned food. Eventually he will come out on the coast and take passage to Martinique on a French gunboat. His contempt for the natives and their hopes of capturing him is boundless, for he is a civilized man and their inevitable superior. Amidst his boasts, the distant tomtoms, the voice of the natives, become audible, and speed him on his way. Jones is not entirely exempt from awe and terror at the thought of heathen magic, but he puts on a bold face for Smithers and declares himself as good as in Martinique.

By nightfall, Jones has travelled as far as the beginning of the Great Forest. He is nervous, tired and footsore, but most of all he is hungry. He uncovers the hole where he had hidden the food, but it is not under the white marker stone. In a panic, he realizes that the area is scattered with white stones, and he rushes from one to another, heaving them up. At last he gives up the search as hopeless and turns to face the forest. But when he does, he sees his own Little Formless Fears objectified before him as dark, mocking shadows with beady eyes, hiding behind the trees. He is terrified and at once fires a shot at them. The apparitions vanish and Jones enters the forest.

In the midst of the forest, Jones comes upon a second apparition, that of Jeff, the Negro he had killed in a gambling quarrel. By now, Jones has lost his imperial aplomb. His hat has disappeared, his clothes are torn in several places and his face is scratched. At first he does not realize that Jeff is a ghost, but when he does, his reaction is violent and frenzied. He shoots at the figure which immediately disappears, leaving him alone with the ever-increasing tempo of the tomtoms. In his haste to escape, he plunges into the underbrush, forgetting the path.

Next he stumbles out of the forest onto a road, burning with heat and fright. He rips off his coat and spurs impatiently, and wonders aloud whether the ghost he saw was the result of his weakened condition or was indeed real. Even as he speaks, the third apparition is before him: a Negro chain gang working on the road, followed by a white prison guard bearing a whip. The guard orders the terrified Jones into line, and he obeys without question. The guard whips him, then turns away. Jones raises his imaginary shovel to kill the man, but discovers he has no weapon except his gun. Again he shoots, and again the ghosts vanish.

After another rush through the forest, Jones comes out into a clearing all in tatters and wildly fearful. He throws himself on his knees, repenting all his sins in a frantic prayer and begging for help. He tears off his ruined shoes and throws them away, ruefully regarding their loss as a sign that he has sunk to his lowest point. When he looks up, he sees yet another apparition, that of an auction block surrounded by southern gentry. It is himself that they are bidding for, and Jones goes wild with rage and fear. He shoots at his tormentors and suddenly he is alone.

He next appears in a tiny clearing reminiscent of a ship's hold, and indeed there are two rows of Negroes sitting chained together, wailing, on their way to slavery. In his terror, Jones sways with their rhythm and his voice joins theirs, even rising above the others. This apparition leaves him of itself and he rushes off, to appear next at the foot of a great tree by a river. Here there is a pile of rocks resembling an altar, before which Jones kneels, as if hypnotized. He is dimly aware of having been in the place before. As he watches, a witchdoctor appears, dancing in pantomime the god's demand for a sacrifice. Jones sees that the sacrifice demanded is himself and cries for mercy. The witchdoctor conjures up a crocodile which lies on the bank, looking hungrily at Jones. Though the witchdoctor motions him toward the monster, Jones resists, and fires his last shot, the silver bullet, to make the crocodile and the witchdoctor disappear. Jones falls prone on the ground, paralyzed with fear while the tomtoms continue their inexorable rhythms.

Smithers stands with the natives and their leader, Lem, at the beginning of the forest line where Jones sought his buried food. Lem's soldiers carry rifles that have silver bullets made from melted coins. Smithers expresses great scorn for their efforts and declares himself certain that Jones has escaped. But there are sounds of shots in the forest that send Lem's riflemen out among the trees. More shots follow and the tomtoms cease. The soldiers return, carrying Jones' body. Smithers mocks Jones briefly for his ignominious end, but even as he mocks he admires the man who would not die until killed with silver bullets.

THE EMPEROR JONES

CHARACTER ANALYSIS

SMITHERS

Smithers is a crafty and unscrupulous trader who has made his living by tricking the natives and has found his master in Jones, his onetime apprentice. Smithers' attitude toward the natives is one of contempt and callousness, and he strongly desires to regard Jones the same way. Throughout the play, he fights his conviction of inferiority to the Negro Emperor, at the same time feeling a sense of awe and respect for his ability.

BRUTUS JONES

Brutus Jones appears from the beginning of the play as a man who has collided with the most unpleasant facts of life and has forced them to work to his advantage. There is a sense of the comic about him; he continually makes light of the trappings that surround him as Emperor, and he refuses at first to take his difficulties seriously. Yet we never cease to feel respect for this powerful, ruthless and utterly practical man who has risen from pullman porter to Emperor. He is not hysterical in the least. When later in the play he begins to have hallucinations and to break down, we do not lay these disorders to any innate instability in his character or to an excess of imaginative sensibility.

Comment

The manner in which the Emperor Jones died is, in one sense, a vindication of his attitude of pride throughout the play. From the beginning he appears as a man not only royal in name but also possessed by a belief in his own superiority over the natives and his accomplice, Smithers. For ten years, Jones declares, he served white men as a train porter, and he learned from them how to steal on a grand scale. Jones identifies himself proudly with the white man as he knew him, and imitates the worst and most cynical behavior of his former masters. He cherishes no illusions about the value of his throne. To him it is merely a means to the accumulation of money which will free him from all servitude and bondage forever. As Emperor, he declares, the law does not apply to him. He is beyond the reach of the primitives around him because of their fear and his silver charm. The bullet represents the first element of savagery apparent in Jones' character. When he speaks of the luck it brings him against all the lesser breeds of men, the tomtoms begin and frighten him. Throughout the play they maintain the **theme** of savagery and of the compelling hold of the primitive life.

In the scenes of Jones' flight from the natives, there are distinct degrees of regression on his part to that very savagery he believes himself to be escaping. His fate is fixed by his biological inheritance of fear, slavery, criminality and greed. Just as he throws off his clothes, remnants of civilization which are burdensome to a man fighting for survival, he gradually throws off the sophistication of an American tough. The darkness comes upon him early in his flight and intensifies his fears, reducing them to the level of the childlike or primitive mind. With every shot he directs at the apparitions that arise to haunt him, Jones reverts more irrevocably into his own past and into that of his race. At first his visions are only of the two murders he committed. He banishes them with the whiteman's weapon, each bullet fired clearing his mind of one horror that the next may engulf it. After relieving his personal sins, Jones experiences a resurgence of the religion that before had been only a matter of form. As usual, he approaches life directly, without dreams, hopes or myths to sustain him; his prayer is for forgiveness so that he may receive material aid.

Religion, however, proves inadequate to dam the flood of his racial memories or to release the hold they have gained upon him. His visions of the slave market and the hold of the slave ship sink him deeper into the Negro past, returning him psychologically to Africa. On the auction block he is defiant, still considering himself a free man, but when he joins the slaves in the hold, he sings their dirge as one of them. His pride is humbled; he is aware of his wretchedness. This apparition of the slaves in the hold is the only one not blasted with a bullet. Instead, it is merely terminated in darkness and flight and in the cries of Jones.

This utter prostration is completed by the ritual scene at the sacred tree and stone altar, a primitive cathedral to which Jones is drawn as worshipper and victim, completely without will and in the power of primitive magic represented by the witchdoctor. The crocodile which is to consume him Jones destroys with the silver bullet meant for himself. The reptile has taken, then, the one means by which Jones planned to preserve his dignity from the natives. This marks the completion of his reversion to savagery; his pride is gone; he is sapped of the civilization represented by the gun. During his flight he has circled round and headed back toward the natives he sought to escape. He is drawn toward the tomtoms while his enemies sit and wait for him. In the end, the abyss of savagery opens up and receives the Emperor who thought to escape it forever. Yet he does not entirely lose the dignity inherent in him from the beginning; it is with white, silver bullets that he is shot. He dies on his own terms, not those of the primitive society he dominated.

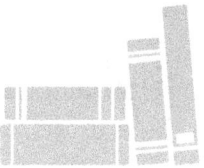

THE EMPEROR JONES

ESSAY QUESTIONS AND ANSWERS

Question: How does O'Neill bring home to the audience the pride of Brutus Jones? How does he show its disintegration?

Answer: Through his own boasting in the palace, Jones reveals himself as a man who feels that laws are not made for him, that intelligent self-interest obliges him to steal from the ignorant and that he is invulnerable to death except on his own terms. His hallucinations in the jungle reinforce this reading of his character. He sees himself at the peak of his power when he committed the two murders. Several times he has agonizing visions of himself in slavery, being tormented by whites, and in these visions he reacts with murderous violence. He does not react this way, however, when he finds himself in the hold of the slave ship. Instead, he feels himself totally one with them in their misery. His pride and dignity break down rapidly after this point, just as his fine clothes disintegrate during the flight. The victory of racial past over individual pride is apparent in our last sight of Jones, prostrate before the stone altar after the apparition of the witchdoctor and the crocodile. This scene is a prelude to his death, the ultimate abasement of pride.

Question: What is Jones' attitude toward religion at the beginning of the play? At the end?

Answer: When Jones is sure of himself and his power, he regards Christianity as a superficial affair which he can take up and put aside at his leisure. He is perfectly willing to participate in native rites if this will contribute to his power over the natives, and he even attributes some slight degree of validity to them. After his first frightening experience in the jungle, however, Jones' feelings about the supernatural change. His primitive fears come to the surface, and against them, he prays fervently for succor to the Christian God. He repents his sins, but at the same time he asks to be delivered from his punishment for them. He is trying to use God just as he has always used people. This prayer fails to save him and his next "religious" experience is a purely primitive one. He cannot help joining in the ritual of the witchdoctor, which is intended to offer him as victim to the evil forces all around him. In religion, as in everything else, Jones has completed the transformation from civilized man to savage.

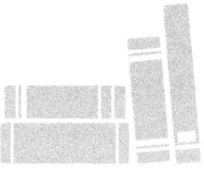

THE HAIRY APE

INTRODUCTION

Eugene O'Neill thought of *The Hairy Ape* as the natural complement or descendent of *The Emperor Jones*. While Jones sinks back into his past, Yank, the ape-like seaman, attempts to rise to a higher level. Not only is the Darwinian idea of evolution dramatized, but also the Emersonian idea of modern man having become mechanized. Emerson, a nineteenth century idealist, felt that man was no longer the master of his machines, but their slave. He is no longer a splendid animal close to the earth like Brutus Jones, but a lost creature bound to nothing but his machine. No longer is man in harmony with nature; he belongs to nothing.

Yank, the hero of the play, is not a unique or sensitive individual. He is a symbol of suffering and baffled humanity, trapped in an age when the worker is becoming irrelevant to the production of goods. He progresses painfully through experiences with religion, socialism and the law. Ultimately he tries to find meaning and purpose in the animal world by freeing a caged gorilla, but this final effort fails also. This despairing picture of modern man offers little hope of redemption or of gradual evolution into a higher form of life.

The Hairy Ape was not intended to produce a realistic effect. It dramatized a philosophy, an idea, and it did so in the same type of symbolic, fantastic terms that were so evident in *The Emperor Jones*. The forecastle of the ship, where Yank and his co-workers sleep, suggests a cage, just as the men's faces and physiques suggest apes. The ceiling is oppressively low, a testimony to the crushing burden borne by these men. The nightmare scene on Fifth Avenue, where the rich move like robots from their church, vividly represents the indifference of the powerful toward the poor and toward the higher implications of their religion. In the eight quickly shifting scenes of the play, the destiny of the common man in our time is symbolically worked out as an unrelieved tragedy.

Eugene O'Neill had drawn the idea behind *The Hairy Ape* from real life. An ex-shipmate of his named Driscoll committed suicide, and O'Neill began imagining the causes of this act, as did others who had known Driscoll. It seemed to him that Driscoll had ceased to feel that he "belonged," and that this sense was common to most modern men. O'Neill did not want people to think he was simply trying to win sympathy for sailors or for a depressed class of workers. His message was for all men: that we are struggling to "belong" and that this can never happen until we can find in ourselves the missing quality of understanding. O'Neill indicated in a letter that "life in itself is nothing," and that man's glory lies in his struggle to fulfill his dreams of a better and a nobler existence, even though the struggle is hopeless. In order to do this, he must first "know himself," as the Greeks thought, and accept the truths about himself that he has learned. Yank's initial crisis is seeing himself unfavorably in the mirror of the society girl when she calls him a "filthy beast." After this incident, and throughout the play, he struggles to find out exactly who and what he is. He is unwilling to accept the judgment that he is a "beast," but he is no longer secure in his manly pride as a stoker.

A crowd of apelike, dirty seamen are enjoying their time off in the cage-like, jammed quarters of a liner's forecastle. They are nearly all drunk, and their noisy singing and cursing suggests the elemental fury of caged beasts. The men seem to feel a basic unity with one another, and to "belong" to their group, without being consciously aware of the fact. In their simplicity, they cannot be said to be aware of much of anything beyond the pleasure of drink and congenial companions. Yank, the most powerful and belligerent of them all, is recognized as the group's spokesman, the ultimate representative of a type. He is their symbol.

There is a jumble of loud talk. It is not true conversation, but simple phrases or ejaculations. The men are not really interested in communicating anything. Yank, however, cuts into all this with a burst of real human speech, primitive and ungrammatical as it is. He is scornful of them and all they say, and this attitude of rejection and criticism is characteristic of him throughout the play.

The men ask Paddy, a "monkey-like" old Irishman, to sing, and his pathetic song is an old sea chanty from sailing ship days. Yank heaps scorn upon any relic of the old days, declaring the song "dead," and the singer dead with it. He cries for silence so he can "t'ink." As often happens throughout the play, the rest cry out in metallic tones this one word "t'ink," which is so alien to them that they are forced to express their dumb shock in a united chorus.

A sentimental singer begins a romantic song, which Yank cuts off as he did the other with a burst of bitterness against "dat tripe." Home, love and women are meaningless words for him. A sailor named Long, a socialist, makes an impassioned speech against the capitalist exploiters, but Yank shouts him down also.

He sees himself as far more important to the maintenance of civilization than are the industrialists, for he fuels the machines. He declares, in his pride, that he and those like him "belong" while the parasites do not. Paddy contests this in a long, mournful speech about the clean old days on the sailing ships, when machines did not dehumanize sailors and make them slaves. But Yank, enraged, declares that he and not Paddy is the real spokesman of man. He is the one who feeds the machine as one feeds a child, and who is made even more powerful by the machine. When the call comes to go back to work, Paddy is too drunk to go, and Yank strides out with dynamic contempt and self-confidence to feed his machine.

Mildred Douglas, pale aristocratic daughter of a steel magnate, is reclining with her aunt on the upper deck. The two contrast with the beauty of the sea and ship, both being highly artificial, life-drained creatures. Mildred has been to college and has been a social worker, but she is bored and wants new experiences to give meaning to her anemic way of life. She is going to inspect the English poor, and her aunt accuses her spitefully of seeking thrills. Mildred protests she really wants to help the poor, but has no more vitality. She is simply a played-out, "waste product" of the industrial process, Mildred declares. She and her aunt clearly hate each other and when Mildred goes off with the Second Engineer to inspect the laborers in the stokehole, she gives her aunt an insulting slap across the cheek.

After having seen Yank and his fellows at play, we now view them in the blazing furnace room, where they labor like chained animals, moving mechanically like the machine they are feeding. Yank rises above all the exhausted men, urging them on to greater efforts, shouting that they should all fill the monster furnace not because the engineers says so but because it is their "baby." As he shouts, Mildred and two engineers appear. He does not see them in his rage at the constant, inhuman blasts of the whistle demanding that they put in more fuel. His shouted threats at the engineers above who run the whistle are in contrast to the silence of the others who see Mildred. At last Yank turns and glares at her and she cowers in disgust, calling him a beast. She is helped out, fainting, while Yank curses and throws his shovel at the door that has just slammed behind her.

Yank is brooding in the forecastle, taunted by his fellows for being in love. He declares that he has "fallen in hate," and that he will get vengeance for his humiliation. He is even more incensed to learn that Mildred belongs to the family that owns steel, and thus the ships and ultimately himself. His pride in himself is shattered to learn that she came to view him like a beast in the zoo. He threatens to murder her, saying that she doesn't "belong," and that she isn't even alive compared to him. He plans to show her that his brute strength is more human and valuable than her social status.

Three weeks later, Yank and Long appear in front of a Fifth Avenue jewelry store. They are waiting for the rich to come out of the church. Long has brought Yank here to view the elite, with the hope of converting him to socialism. While Long declaims against the jewelry and fine buildings, Yank expresses child-like admiration. He is furious, however, at seeing monkey pelts in a furrier's window. He feels a kinship with beasts slaughtered for the convenience of the rich. As the modish crowd leaves the church, more like puppets than flesh-and-blood people, they comment mechanically on the minister's sermon. When Yank tries to insult them, they treat him as if he is not there. Afraid of violence, Long sneaks away, leaving Yank to attack the whole class in a frenzy. He is at least able to attract the attention of one man, who only notices him because Yank has made him miss his bus. This gentleman calls the police, who beat Yank up and carry him off. In jail Yank tells the other prisoners that he and all of them are apes. The others sympathize with the story of his humiliation and urge him to blow up the capitalists as the Industrial Workers of the World are trying to do. The I.W.W. was a socialist group that in the late 1890s attempted to weld all workers into one huge union. Yank tries to join the group but the leaders see that he is simply a frenzied anarchist and throw him out. Once again Yank is rejected.

The next day Yank goes to the monkey house at the zoo. The gorilla's brute strength impresses him and he speaks to the animal as a friend. He describes the feelings he had in the park, watching the sun rise on the sea. At last he understood Paddy's nostalgia for the old life, but he knew he could never belong to it. This realization led him to seek out the gorilla. Yank says the gorilla is lucky to belong to one world while he belongs to neither heaven nor earth. Identifying himself with the animal, Yank frees him to get even with the men who have put him in the cage. The gorilla picks him up, crushes him and throws him into the open cage. When the door has slammed shut on him and the gorilla has gone, the dying Yank calls out mockingly to imaginary spectators to step right up and have a look at the "one and only-Hairy Ape." He dies, having pronounced this final judgment on himself. In a stage note the playwright suggests that perhaps Yank "at last belongs."

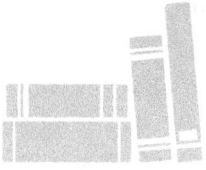

THE HAIRY APE

CHARACTER ANALYSIS

ROBERT SMITH ("YANK")

From our first introduction to him, we understand that Yank is a powerful man, the ultimate laborer, the best of his breed. At the beginning of the play, Yank is sublimely confident that brute strength is the highest standard of human value, and on this conviction he bases his manly pride. Once this idea is shattered, Yank becomes "self-conscious," his simplicity is gone forever. He is no longer at home in the world, and by his death he dramatizes this fact. Because he has always depended on his physical strength, Yank has no other solution for his problems. Mildred hurt him, so he wants to kill her. The rich men snub him, so he attacks them physically. He senses dimly that industry is responsible for his misery, so he plans to blow up the steel factories. Ultimately, he frees the gorilla because of his own urge for action and vengeance. The violence of the gorilla is an ironic and appropriate answer to Yank's obsession with brute strength. Yank lived in and through violence, and so he died by it.

PADDY

The voice of Paddy, throughout the play, is one of detached yet mournful commentary on the action. Paddy knows that his world is dead and that it was the only one worth living in. His sad songs reveal his nostalgia for the lost way of life that was truly human. His affirmation of human values, however diluted it may be by drink, stands in dramatic contrast to Yank's rejection of every value but brute force. Paddy's wizened, aged body is also a graphic contrast to Yank's powerful one. Paddy sees clearly that his fellows are slaves to the machines, and that only ruin can come from this caged, hideous existence. At the very end of the play, Yank is able to appreciate Paddy's commitment to the old way of life, though he cannot share it. Thus, Paddy's contribution to the play is that his point of view is the one wholesome and humane possibility for men. Unfortunately, that possibility no longer exists for mankind in the industrialized world of *The Hairy Ape*.

LONG

Far more articulate than Yank, and committed to a cause, Long does not appear as a strongly sympathetic or unique individual. He is only a "type"; he is a talker, but when it comes to action, he is quick to back down. He shows feeling for the poor, which Yank cynically rejects. Like Paddy, Long is raised above the other stokers by virtue of his sense that he "belongs." Yank belonged too, but after Mildred's attack on his pride, he belonged no more. Long tries to help Yank belong to socialism, but Yank is too fiercely individualistic to accept such a solution.

MILDRED DOUGLAS

Though she expresses interest in the poor, Mildred is made impotent to act on her convictions because of her bloodless aristocratic background. She always wears white, a symbol of her spiritual anemia. In seeking out the stokehole and the slums, Mildred is trying to link herself in some positive way with the more vital elements of humanity, uncorrupted by money or power. Her hope is clearly that she may gain strength and vigor from associating with them, just as factories and ships gain their power from the labor of men like Yank.

Comment

From the very first scene, we are made aware that the men of Yank's class have lost their roots in the earth and even in the sea. Paddy's doleful remarks about the old way of life emphasize this tragic condition. Long's socialist diatribes pose one solution, but it is far too impersonal and remote to appeal to a simple fellow like Yank. He finds all his happiness in his union with the machine, though Paddy says this is a bad sign. To Yank, the machine is a baby, to be fed and even loved. His power stems from the feeling that he runs the world from his stokehole. Without him, industrial empires would crumble. In this way he can believe he "belongs" to the modern world and has a stake in it. The furnace is Yank's manhood. Paddy declares that this is very different from being united with the sea and the ship in the old days. One may belong to the mysterious and the beautiful in nature, but not to a filthy, ugly, dead world and he to a living one when all the men except the drunken Paddy leave for their shift at the furnace.

Like Yank, Mildred Douglas sees herself as part of a machine. She says she is simply a "waste product in the Bessemer process." Unlike Yank, she is aware that this union with the machine is tragic, and she attempts to do something about it. Her efforts are futile, however, and we last see her in a state of collapse upon being confronted with real life. Her sense of superiority, so evident on the sunny decks, is destroyed by a glimpse of the brutality of real life. Her faint is a kind of death; she is a frail, white candle, extinguished by the great blasts from the furnace that we have learned to identify with Yank.

At first Yank is angry only at Mildred, seeing her as a person, not as a class. She has destroyed his sense of his own worth, and it is she that must be destroyed. As he thinks the matter over, throughout the rest of the play, he gradually learns that the whole world pronounces the same judgment on him that Mildred does. He can only learn this by leaving the stokehole to go among the rich, the revolutionary poor and finally, the animals. In his progress through society he rejects all the possible solutions to the problem of his identity: law, government, religion, social revolution and love. These things are all beyond him and he knows it. He wishes to destroy them in his helpless fury because they emphasize the hopelessness of his search to belong.

Because human society has failed him utterly, Yank finally turns to communion with the animal world. He sees himself without a past or a future, only in a present to which he can never belong. He feels the gorilla has been caged because he enjoys a harmonious state of mind. He wants the gorilla to join him a battle against humanity. By having the gorilla kill Yank, O'Neill suggests that there simply is no home anywhere for men such as Yank in the modern world.

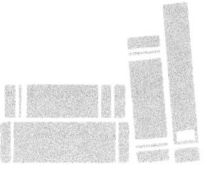

THE HAIRY APE

ESSAY QUESTIONS AND ANSWERS

Question: How do men seek to "belong" in *The Hairy Ape*? Who in the play succeeds in belonging and how?

Answer: Of the stokers, Paddy and Long belong respectively to the values of the past and to the revolutionary socialist commitment to the future. Paddy's life is reduced to impotence and Long's is productive only of words and emotions, not deeds. Yank initially belongs to the machine world, but he loses this sense of belonging early in the play, and only regains it, tentatively, by his death. Mildred belongs to the aristocracy, but she longs to escape this identification. Her failure to do so is reflected in her leaving a position as a social worker and her faint in the furnace room. Ultimately, she, like Yank, is caught between two worlds, unable to reconcile them or belong to either completely.

Question: Are there any genuine personal relationships in the play? Discuss Mildred's relationship with her aunt. Discuss Yank's with Mildred and with his co-workers.

Answer: O'Neill felt that man's main problem was his lack of understanding of his fellow man. This lack was responsible for the sense of being lost that marks nearly all the characters in the play. One cannot belong with other people unless one, in some sense, belongs to them and feels sympathy with them. Because no one in the play was able to feel this sense of shared interest and commitment with another person, not one of the characters is capable of genuinely understanding another.

Mildred rejected her aunt not merely as a person, but as a representative of the class whose limitations Mildred felt she had to escape. Her aunt is not even given a name. Mildred does not try to understand or to share their common background with the older woman. Instead she humiliates her and mocks her as she would a servant. In rejecting her aunt's company for that of the stokers she performs an act that is symbolic and not truly personal. Mildred comes the closest to recognizing another human being as a real person when she encounters Yank. The immediacy and violence of this experience is too much for her and she faints.

Yank at first regards Mildred and her opinion of him as a personal and not impersonal matter. His pride is wounded deeply because this is so. His hatred for Mildred is the closest he comes to an emotional response toward another person. Toward his co-workers Yank displays indifference. Paddy is capable of noble feelings, but he is too old to reach Yank. Long's commitment is to an ideology, not to persons, and he leaves Yank cold. Finally, Yank is able to feel warmth and friendship, but not toward a person. He reaches out instead to a gorilla, projecting his own emotions onto the animal. In loving the gorilla, he is actually only loving a reflection of himself. Throughout his experience he has tragically failed to understand and accept personally any other human being. The most he can achieve is a partial understanding of himself and his predicament. For a man like Yank, however, this is an heroic achievement and we are led to feel sympathy and sorrow for the man who accomplished it.

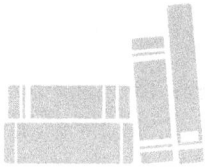

DESIRE UNDER THE ELMS

INTRODUCTION

The hatred that sometimes exists between father and son was a matter of personal experience for Eugene O'Neill, as well as being a tenet of the Freudian psychology which dominated the playwright's time. For O'Neill, Freudian psychology, with its emphasis on the attachment between mother and son, and hostility between son and father, reinforced the inner meaning of the Greek tragedies with their fascination for incest. Adler, another influential twentieth century psychologist, felt that the will to power, not incest, was the central drive of men, and his conclusions also influenced O'Neill in the composition of the play. The sons long to possess the patrimony of their father, and their hatred of him is largely caused by his authority over them due to his possession of the farm. *Desire Under the Elms* reflects this hatred in strong, elemental, dramatic terms.

The country people of *Desire Under the Elms* are by no means the pure, simple, joyous pagans of classical literature. They are aware of their unity with things of the earth, but they are also aware of their seething inner drives and passions. The woman, Abbie, is the very land itself; she embraces the lives of each one of the characters in the play. The religious attitudes presented in the play are not the simple pagan ones of classical literature. The father confuses himself with a narrowly-conceived, harsh, Old Testament Jehovah. The animal longing of others in the play for a simple life with its simple pleasures clashes disastrously with the God-complex of the grim old man who possesses and will not share.

In *Desire Under the Elms*, O'Neill's straightforward determinism gave way to a more profound awareness of the hidden and unchartable depths within individual men. Characters are not so much dominated by their social and economic circumstances as they were in *The Hairy Ape* and *Anna Christie*. Instead, their fate is determined by the universal and timeless passions that drive them from within. These passions and their fulfillment often clash with the prevailing ethics of western society.

For his apparent championing of natural desires over the puritan code, O'Neill was much criticized when *Desire Under the Elms* was produced. During the play's first run at the Greenwich Village Theater in New York City, a city official tried to have it condemned and taken off the stage. He succeeded only in advertising the play as one which pure people should not see. Naturally everyone wanted to see the play, and they found that the tragedy was not spicy, but somber and even moralistic, in its own peculiar way. O'Neill had achieved a fusion of tragic grandeur with simplicity of character and language. The mythic and timeless atmosphere of the play is enhanced by its setting in the mid-nineteenth century past. In the isolated New England farmhouse of the Cabot family, there exists a self-contained universe, where the elemental human relationships become clear in their attraction or opposition to each other.

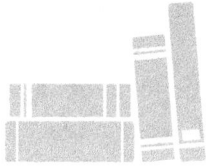

DESIRE UNDER THE ELMS

CHARACTER ANALYSIS

EPHRAIM CABOT:

Like many other fathers in the plays of Eugene O'Neill, Ephraim is a man incapable of showing love. His inability is not merely a New England cultural trait, but a universal masculine difficulty made extreme for dramatic purposes. A man like Ephraim fears to show love because he fears being "soft." To him, being a man is being hard enough to possess his world without question as to his authority. At several points in the play his love for Abbie seems to have mellowed him and made him able, for the first time in his life, to communicate his feelings. It is too late, however, for he is far too old for Abbie to love him as he loves her. When he loses Abbie he no longer cares to keep the farm, because for him she had become the farm.

SIMEON AND PETER:

These two older sons of Ephraim are in their late thirties. They are almost alike for the purposes of the play, with one exception: Simeon recalls the presence of his dead wife with nostalgia and

Peter is indifferent to such feelings. The two older brothers are thick, dirty and intended to seem like contented, uncomplicated animals. In the play, such a character is viewed as a distinct virtue, something everyone should strive for. Their dislike for their father accentuates and makes believable Eben's hatred, for we are led to believe we can trust the simple instincts of Simeon and Peter. Their hatred, however, is not as intense as Eben's, and they are released to find freedom early in the play.

EBEN CABOT:

Eben is a handsome young man in his mid-twenties. His dark eyes remind one of a caged animal's and his expression is resentful and hostile. He gives the impression of "repressed vitality"; that is to say, he is fighting his instincts and is thus unhappy. He is bound to his mother who represents the farm for him, and his driving desire is to take for his own all that is his father's. By doing this he hopes to take vengeance on Ephraim for his callous treatment of Eben's mother.

ABBIE PUTNAM:

Abbie is a powerful, aggressive woman in her midthirties, whose instincts are fully in control of her life. She is driven by a passion for a home that she can possess entirely. Once she comes to represent the farm, that is, once she has absorbed it and made it totally her own, she reaches out to possess Eben also. She becomes both farm and mother at the same time. Her passion for Eben is part of her passion for home. She knows that Eben is his mother's heir, as he does, even though Ephraim does not always acknowledge the fact. She must unite with Eben to possess the farm entirely.

Comment

PART I

We first see the Cabot home under the domination of the elms. The trees are a feminine symbol, and ultimately they become a symbol for Abbie. As the elms dominate the house, so she comes to dominate it also, and with it the whole family. She does not do this until the ghost of Eben's mother is laid to rest by his act of defiance with Abbie in Part II. From the second scene of Part I on, we are aware that Eben is haunted by his mother's ghost which broods over the entire house. He feels it is his responsibility to satisfy his mother by destroying his father. One way he accomplishes this is by courting the village prostitute, Min, who was courted by his father also. He takes a savage pleasure in possessing a woman who was once his father's. This urge sets the stage for his attraction to his new step-mother, making it all the more believable. His second great act of defiance is to send away Simeon and Peter, his older competitors and his father's useful workhorses. This is a direct blow at his father's power over the farm and when he succeeds in getting rid of them, Eben feels the farm is even more his own.

PART II

Now there are only three participants in the action, father, mother and son. The son, Eben, has arranged matters so that he alone remains to fight it out with his father for possession of the farm and Abbie.

Abbie sees Eben as the image of his father and it is through her that we are helped to understand that much of the hostility between father and son is their likeness to one another. Though

Eben hates to think of himself as Ephraim's son, the fact is that his whole life is built around his desire to take over Ephraim's identity as his own. Abbie presents a threat not merely because she wants the farm herself, but because she wants to dominate Eben and make him warm and earthy like herself, not cold, lonely and inhuman like Empraim. This explains much of the source of Eben's initial hostility to Abbie. Ephraim also perceives the identity between son and father. He softens momentarily towards Eben when he considers that if his son inherits the property, it still, in a sense, belongs to the father. This impulse is quickly stilled, however, when Abbie promises him a new son. Since he sees her as the incarnation of the farm, a son by her has a double significance.

Just as Ephraim resents Eben's claim on the farm, Eben resents Abbey for taking his mother's place as the real possessor of the farm. Only by making love to Abbie is a new attitude toward the farm born in him. Now Abbie becomes his mother to him and at last he feels himself possessor of both farm and mother. He feels that he and his mother have finally had their vengeance upon Ephraim.

PART III

The birth of a son to Eben confuses him. He resents the baby's likeness to him, just as he and Ephraim resent each other. In his rage at Abbie's supposed betrayal, his unconscious hostility appears openly and he wishes the baby dead. Abbie feels that her relationship to her son-lover Eben is more important than her relationship to the baby. Eben wishes she had killed Ephraim instead and is enraged because she took his son from him. All his life, he feels, what is his has been taken by another. For Eben, this is Abbie's ultimate betrayal and he gets revenge by betraying her to the sheriff. In the end the two lovers overcome the merely animal aspect of their love. Eben is able to forgive Abbie and assume half the blame for the crime himself. The attitude of Eben and Abbie at the end is one of gentle and "devout" harmony with the world and its ways even when they are doomed by them.

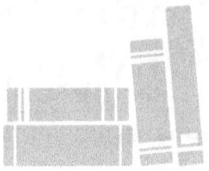

DESIRE UNDER THE ELMS

ESSAY QUESTIONS AND ANSWERS

1. What two moral codes are apparent in the play? To which code does Ephraim adhere? To which does Abbie? Which does O'Neill seem to condemn?

The code of a puritanical form of Christianity wars with the joyful pagan ideal of enjoyment of nature and instinct throughout the play. Ephraim Cabot identifies himself with the strict God of justice in the Old Testament. He is also dedicated to the puritan tradition, which is commonly understood as the repression of all feelings and the doing of one's duty at all costs. Ephraim's hardness, so necessary to his success in a hard, lonely world, isolated him from other people and prevented him from loving or being loved. Abbie, on the other hand, rejoiced in the expression of love and found her personal fulfillment in an uninhibited union with the land and her lover, Eben. O'Neill leaves little doubt that Abbie's attitude has more genuine religious and humane content than does Ephraim's.

2. In what three main ways does Eben defy his father? Why did Eben feel driven to these acts of defiance?

Early in the play Eben drives away the cowlike mainstays of his father's farm, Simeon and Peter. Without them the father is alone and much less powerful. Eben's second act of defiance was his selection of Min, his father's old mistress, as the object for his romantic attentions. Eben's last and greatest act of defiance was making love to his father's wife, Abbie. Each one of these acts was motivated by Eben's desire to take his father's place. Though Eben's father is left alive and still in possession of the farm at the end, Eben is the real victor of the struggle. He and Abbie leave the farm to Ephraim, in a final joint act of defiance, and Ephraim finds that the farm no longer means anything to him.

3. What did Abbie represent for Ephraim? For Eben?

Abbie, in her earthiness, strength and obstinacy, represented to old Ephraim the farm he had loved and labored at for so long. For the first time, he was able to express his love and to hold another person higher than himself. Abbie could demand anything from him and get it, whereas his other wives and his sons had found that asking him for anything was like trying to get blood from a stone. Ephraim had never been satisfied with his sons by other women. It was only by Abbie that he could have a son who would be a true son of the farm and himself.

Eben viewed Abbie in a more complex fashion. She was more than the farm to him. She was the resurrected presence of his mother as well. Only by making love to her, can he put his mother's memory aside for a vital, living relationship. In desiring so overwhelmingly to possess the land, Eben was also desiring to be the only man in his mother's life, and he succeeded in this ambition by becoming Abbie's lover.

STRANGE INTERLUDE

INTRODUCTION

O'Neill settled down in Bermuda to write the first half of *Strange Interlude* in the spring of 1926. That summer, vacationing in Maine, he worked on the second half. During the writing of the play, he read several works of Freud and consulted a psychoanalyst on certain technical points in his psychological drama. Freudian analysis was not the only source O'Neill drew upon in the writing of *Strange Interlude*. Schopenhauer, the pessimistic German philosopher of the nineteenth century, influenced O'Neill's idea that love was rooted in basic sex instincts and that life was at the mercy of chance.

Strange Interlude was finished in 1927 and produced in 1928, just at the time O'Neill's marriage to Agnes was breaking up. Despite the play's incredible length (it ran from 5:30 to 11:00 P.M. with eighty minutes out for dinner), it was a great box office success, and won O'Neill still another Pulitzer Prize.

A central theme of the play is the conflict between the demands of reality and the romantic illusions through which people view reality. O'Neill dramatizes this conflict through the device of the "aside." A character will say one thing to his companion and show his real feelings in an aside, speaking out loud for the benefit of the audience. From the beginning, Nina Leeds, the heroine, is dominated by her romantic dream of Gordon Shaw. Her father, Marsden, and Darrell all fight against the reality of life in one way or another. Gordon and Sam Evans are the only men in Nina's life who approach reality directly and powerfully. People like Gordon succeed at life, the others suffer or gain only temporary happiness.

The "interlude" of the title refers to the period between Nina's girlhood and her late thirties, that is, the time when she is a beautiful and desirable woman. Before this period, Nina was secure and happy in her retired life with her father. Afterwards, she presumably experiences an equally secure, passionless and uncomplicated life with the father-figure, Charles Marsden. The interlude is a time of tragic upset and confusion, during which Nina is obsessed with the idea of "God as Mother," that is, God as vitality, fertility and action. In the end, she is cast aside by her son for another woman, just as she cast her father aside.

STRANGE INTERLUDE

CHARACTER ANALYSIS

PROFESSOR HENRY LEEDS:

Small, slender and with delicate features, the professor has an air of puritanical primness about him. He is timid by temperament, but behaves in a superior manner, as if the world at large were his classroom. His scholarly interests are all in the ancient past, and he is afraid of real life, which Nina and her womanly passions represent. He is able to repent his sin of desiring Gordon Shaw's death only when he sees that he has lost Nina anyway and can even feel relief at her going.

CHARLES MARSDEN:

Like Leeds, the writer Marsden is removed from reality and from sex. He is attached to his mother, that is, to an unobtainable dream. An unfortunate experience with a prostitute in his youth has made him hate and fear the sexual side of love, and he continually manifests this revulsion in his novels and in his personal life. He is afraid to contaminate himself with real life, and cannot bear either to be hated or loved.

NINA LEEDS:

Nina is a beautiful, athletic and passionate girl, whose radiant look belies her inner mental sickness. Her reactions to life are complicated by her over-civilized upbringing. She has difficulty sorting out the real and unreal, romantic illusion and biological fact. She is fated to suffer for her obstinate pursuit of an ideal represented by Gordon Shaw. Throughout the play, Nina is obsessed with a longing to "give herself' because she was prevented from giving herself to Gordon before he died. In return for this "gift" she expects her men to belong only to her. Just as she sacrifices herself for Evans, others must sacrifice themselves for her, since that is the essence of love in the mind of women.

EDMUND DARRELL:

Ned Darrell represents the man of science in the world of *Strange Interlude*. He is cool, observant and analytical, though he must work constantly to control his intensely passionate nature. For Darrell, sex is at first unalluring because he understands it as a merely biological phenomenon. His love for Nina allows his passions to break loose, and he forgets his resolve to live by reason alone. Initially he makes love to her with his highminded motive of service to her and Evans, but he is trapped by his own clinical philosophy.

SAM EVANS:

There is a boyishness about Evans that is later to be evident in his foster son, Gordon. His simplicity, innocence and lack of confidence inspire maternal love, and this love is responsible for his success in life. Evans needs to have his wife become his mother so that he may become a man. He is delighted to share his "mother" with young Gordon, and there is thus no hostility between them. It is only when Nina is a contented mother that Evans can feel secure enough to make a living as a man.

ACT I

The study of Professor Leeds, Nina's father, reveals that this scholar has retreated from reality and is preoccupied with the past. Marsden, the novelist, at once reveals himself as a man who hates and fears sex, and whose love life is centered around his mother. These two men, who are like fathers to Nina, represent to her death, resignation, security and sterility. She has broken away from them because of a third man, Gordon Shaw, who is actually dead but represents life to her.

Comment

Gordon's death set off the entire chain of events that forms Nina's "interlude," and all of these events divide her from her father, who prevented her from fulfilling her love for Gordon. The soldiers in the hospital whom she is going to serve represent Gordon to her. By giving herself to them, Nina will learn to love other men besides her father.

ACT II

Marsden reveals his new identity as Nina's "father," now that Leeds is dead. Nina's year at the hospital has done her little good;

she is still in a state of disintegration and now she is cynical besides. Evans reveals that his love, like Marsden's, is non-fleshly in character, he wants to take care of Nina and does not primarily regard her as a personality in her own right. Marsden is pleased with Evans as a prospective husband for Nina, but he finds Darrell's presence disturbing. Darrell represents the biological side of love, and Marsden, with his poetic-romantic views, must reject all Darrell stands for. Darrell reveals at once that he has not been taken in by the romantic myths that blind the other characters. His judgments on the other characters are intended to be seen as objectively true, almost clinical in their harshness. He sees that Nina must find normal outlets for her craving for sacrifice, instead of pursuing the dead Gordon, and prescribes Evans as a husband. This sin of Darrell's, meddling in human lives, ends in suffering for others as well as himself, and not in happiness. Whenever a man, who is the image of God the Father to Nina, interferes in life, people suffer. Nina feels that the real God of the living is female. The father is a source of punishment and death, but as a mother, Nina tells herself, she will be a source of joy and life.

ACT III

Now that Nina and Evans are married, she has come to replace his mother. The coming of his real mother presents the first crisis of their marriage. Mrs. Evans takes over the act as the real mother figure, who affirms respect for reality and happiness and the essential values in life. Just as Nina is concerned for her unborn child, Mrs. Evans fights for her son, Sammy. For Mrs. Evans, as a mother, the moral code of "God the Father" is less important than the code of the woman, which involves the pursuit of happiness no matter what the cost.

ACT IV

Nina's life with Sam after the loss of their baby again reveals signs of disintegration. Evans feels sterile, cut off from the life and success that marked Gordon Shaw, who was his hero as well as Nina's. Just as Nina gave the professor and Marsden a daughter's love, so she gives Evans, and later their son, a mother's love. Each of the men in the play represents aspects of a woman's life with an ideal man, who for Nina was the lost Gordon Shaw. Nina needs all these men to satisfy the man needs of her complex personality. Chiefly, at this period in her life, she needs a vital, masculine lover, and Ned Darrell takes on this role. It is impossible for him to play the role perfectly until he sees Nina as a person, not as an organism under a microscope. Darrell the scientist, the image of God the Father who causes human tragedy, must be punished for his meddling, and Nina's love is to be the instrument of that punishment.

ACT V

Now that Nina is pregnant with Darrell's child, she has lost her neurotic aspect, and become calm and placid. Life alone is sufficient for her; she has no need to romanticize and falsify reality. She relentlessly forces Darrell to admit he loves her, for she is no longer content with mere dreams. Marsden, with his woe over his dead mother, suddenly comes between the two lovers in time to prevent Nina from breaking up her marriage. The situation repeats the one in which Nina's father came between her and Gordon at the critical moment. Darrell is a man of honor, like Gordon Shaw. He cannot let immediate pleasure overrule his concern for Evans' sanity and his own career. While Nina is concerned to protect those values she now enjoys (her pregnancy and Darrell's love), Darrell thinks beyond them to the code of abstract morality which rules him. When Nina finds she has lost Darrell, she is able to merge her mother-love with a woman's love, that is, she is able to see that her entire responsibility is now Evans' happiness and her child's.

ACT VI

After the birth of the baby he believes is his, Evans can act the role of father and provider. Nina can accept his love as a woman because she at least respects him. Marsden sees Evans as a superficial, active businessman who succeeds out of brashness and insensitivity, but Evans' sane way of life is favorably viewed in the overall judgment of the play and its events. Nina's contentment as Evans' wife is great, because she feels no jealousy; she possesses him absolutely, as both wife and mother. When Darrell returns, ready to claim her, Nina refuses to give up her comfortable position as wife and mother to be only a mistress-wife. She will accept Darrell as a lover only, to be used in rounding out an already full life. At this point in the play, Nina is at her peak; she possesses all three men and her baby as well. From this time on, she begins a gradual disintegration and loss of power over reality.

ACT VII

Nina is aware that she only has a few more years before she is forty, and then she will fade and rot as women do. She is beginning to tire of the struggle for happiness and to want only peace. But she is aware that she has ruined Darrell's life and that forcing him to share her with Evans has corrupted him. Darrell's realizes that he and Nina have suffered a kind of madness so that the healthy, exuberant Evans can enjoy sanity. They both realize that their love has not enriched them but caused them "to rot away in peace." It has even caused young Gordon to turn from them both to Evans, so that Nina no longer possesses her son as she desires. Gordon senses that Darrell is his rival for Nina's love, and his resentment causes him to abandon them both. Nina's love for Darrell and Evans is dying; she has grown to fear and hate the inroads Evans is making on her role as mother to Gordon. Marsden's hope begins to grow strong that he and death will win Nina in the end.

ACT VIII

Though Nina has aged and mentally disintegrated, Darrell has become more youthful. He has gained some fulfillment by staying away from her and devoting himself to science. Nina's last hold on womanhood and love is being loosened. Madeline is taking Gordon from her and she is already mourning. Marsden alone remains to her. Darrell stops her from wrecking Gordon's romance with Madeline.

ACT IX:

Evans is dead and Gordon is bitter toward Nina for not taking better care of him. He feels she has betrayed them both. With a maternal air Madeline helps Gordon not to be harsh with his mother for loving Darrell. Contrasting with their love is that of Nina and Charlie. Charlie wants a peaceful, passionless, fatherly love. The second Gordon has been lost like the first and the completion of the cycle ends the "interlude." Nina returns to the life she knew before Gordon made her a woman.

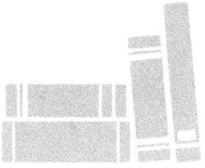

STRANGE INTERLUDE

ESSAY QUESTIONS AND ANSWERS

1. How does the playwright judge the romantic ideal in *Strange Interlude?*

The romantic ideal is seen throughout the play as a disease of life. Darrell, with whom Nina enjoyed the romantic love she might have had with Gordon Shaw, is disillusioned in the last act over the end of his love affair and his shattered career. His futility is emphasized by the fact that his once beloved Nina is now a middle-aged shrew and his son is a materialistic businessman: Nina's hope for happiness is mocked by the loss of young Gordon, who was to be her chief satisfaction in life. Like his father, he is living proof that an active, practical, uncomplicated life triumphs over sensitivity and idealism.

2. Of what does happiness consist, according to the final judgment of the play? Can it be found within the limits of any absolute moral code?

Such happiness as people in *Strange Interlude* are able to gain is found only in the acceptance of reality. To some extent, one can seize what one desires, and this should certainly be done regardless of moral principles, but one is also at the mercy of irrational events.

The moral code, especially the puritan ideal, is chiefly responsible for human misery in the play. Her father's ideals kept Nina from giving herself to Gordon before he was killed, and this forged a whole chain of tragic events. Mrs. Evans tells Nina with the voice of experience, that she would do well to forget the code and find a healthy father for her baby. Nina's resolve to have an abortion and then an affair with Darrell brings her much happiness despite the fact that both deeds are outlawed by the moral code. When Nina obeys the code, as she does by staying with Evans, she must give up her real desire to marry Darrell. The play clearly intends to point out the failure of romantic or moral ideals, indeed of any abstract standards, to solve the complex human problems of the real world.

MOURNING BECOMES ELECTRA

INTRODUCTION

Shortly after their marriage and flight from the United States, Eugene O'Neill and Carlotta Monterey O'Neill leased a splendid chateau near Tours, France. Almost at once (1929) O'Neill began work on his great "trilogy of the damned," as he called it. He claimed that he worked harder and more steadily on this play than on any other up to that time, and it remained his favorite. The last of many revisions was based upon a reading by the actors, during which O'Neill smoothed out the remaining rough spots. After a tryout in Boston, *Mourning Becomes Electra* opened in New York on October 26, 1931. It won the greatest critical reception in modern theatrical history.

One critic felt that the play was too heavily Freudian, but O'Neill argued that writers understood the passions of men and women long before Freud and Jung came on the scene, and that his play could have been written had Freud never lived. Evidence to support this claim can be found in the source of O'Neill's play: Aeschylus' (525-456 B.C.) trilogy about the vengeance of Orestes and Electra upon their own mother for the murder of their father, Agamemnon. Aeschylus dealt with the same themes that fascinated O'Neill, but since Greek classical drama was dominated by the idea that man was controlled by the will of the gods (fate), Aeschylus did not motivate his characters precisely the same way O'Neill was to do. Instead of having his characters pursued by the Furies (godesses of vengeance), O'Neill molds them through heredity and environment. For O'Neill, fate was not the will of the gods, but the past of the individual and his psychological make-up. Thus, fate is an internal force not an external one. Like the plays of the determinist Ibsen, *Mourning Becomes Electra* reveals the behavior of men as conditioned by earlier events in their past. O'Neill made an important change in the pattern established by Aeschylus; instead of basing his play upon Orestes, O'Neill chose Electra (Lavinia) as the main figure, as did the other Greek dramatist who dealt with this myth, Euripides (480-406 B.C.).

The feminine emphasis in *Mourning Becomes Electra* is not an accident; one of the central conflicts of the play is the one between the peaceful worship of the mother and the fatal commitment to the father, which is an attitude associated with the earthy mother goddess, while the 'evil' is the kind of death-in-life. In other words, the 'good' is the free, life-affirming, repressive, puritanical and jealous attitude of the father deity. This same conflict was apparent in *Desire Under the Elms*, where Abbie Putnam pitted her femininity against the 'righteousness' of Ephraim Cabot.

The sin of the Mannon men is their treatment of the *mother;* it is essentially a sin against all that women stand for. Since O'Neill meant Mannon to mean man in general (like the medieval morality play *Everyman)*, we must see the sin of the Mannons and its punishment in universal terms. The Mannons are guilty simply because they exist, and not because of a particularly bloody crime against society. The Greeks would not have understood this idea, for it did not develop until after their time.

In fact, it is influenced by the Christian concept of original sin. The punishment for the Mannons' crime of existence is death, and all the main characters seek death in one way or another. O'Neill's preoccupation with death in *Mourning Becomes Electra* forms a definite conclusion to the themes of all the previous plays. He had suggested other answers to the meaning of life; this play found the meaning of life in death. After *Mourning Becomes Electra*, the universe of Eugene O'Neill stands constructed, and from this point on, his plays tend to reveal an indifference to positive values of any kind.

MOURNING BECOMES ELECTRA

CHARACTER ANALYSIS

EZRA MANNON:

A stiff, grizzled, aloof military man, Ezra Mannon has never allowed himself to express emotion. His manner is abrupt and his voice hollow and commanding. After a lifetime preoccupation with death, he is at last able to express his longing for love and life to Christine. But by the time he apears in the play, death has completely claimed him; he is severed from the sources of life Christine represents.

CHRISTINE MANNON:

From the beginning of the play Christine is regarded as an "outsider" by the townspeople who comment on the action. She, like the French Canadian Marie Brantôme, is "furrin lookin' and queer." It is mentioned that Christine is of French and Dutch descent and that she was poor, which further links her with Marie Brantôme. She looks younger than her forty years, and moves with an animal grace reminiscent of Marie, who was uninhibited and feminine. Christine always wears green, which emphasizes her oneness with nature and fertility, besides setting off her thick, curly bronze hair. Her face is not beautiful, but stunningly handsome in a strong sensual way and it is marked by the mask-like, still expression that all the Mannons and those associated with them wear.

LAVINIA MANNON:

Only twenty-three, Lavinia looks years older. Though her hair and features strongly resemble her mother's, Lavinia does all she can to imitate her father. She is stiff and commanding like him, and always wears black to enhance her likeness to Ezra. Her body is angular, flat-chested and altogether unwomanly. Not until her mother and father are dead can Lavinia begin to develop as a feminine personality in her own right, and to express love. Her hatred of her mother is due to her feeling that she has never experienced love because of Christine's cold attitude toward her. Lavinia's life is further complicated by the fact that her father allows her to vie with Christine for his affection. Until the last play, Lavinia's love for men (including Orin and perhaps Brant) is conditioned by her love for her father, which she transfers to men resembling him. Only when she "becomes" Christine is she able to love the native and Peter Niles, who are distinctly non-Mannon types.

ORIN MANNON:

Hated by his father for coming between husband and wife, Orin drew closer to his mother from childhood on. War forced him to become more like his father and able to murder Brant. Basically, his temperament is sensitive and romantic like his mother's, though facially he strongly resembles Ezra. Like Lavinia, he also looks older than his twenty years, and has assumed the stiff, military bearing of his father. Orin has been manipulated by the three other members of his family all his life and is the weakest of the Mannons. Not until his parents are dead and Lavinia has become feminine like Christine, does Orin assert his masculine prerogatives as head of the family. It is he who determines his sister's destiny in the last act, and not she who controls his.

ADAM BRANT:

Brant is a tall, physically powerful sea captain, who takes care to dress with foppish extravagance, and who cultivates a romantic, almost poetic appearance. His character is not stable; by turns he is weak and strong, manipulated by women and then manipulating other men. He is not at home in life, but is always fighting against it. Dominated by his passion for Christine and his desire for vengeance against Ezra, Brant senses that he is controlled by events. It is this control that he violently and unsuccessfully resists. His desire for freedom and peace is expressed by his longing for the Blessed Isles and for Christine, who represents his mother.

Comment

HOMECOMING. ACT I:

The house of the Mannons wears a "mask" just as all the Mannons are described as having mask-like faces. The ugly house has been given a white temple facade, which hides its basic character. With both the house and the Mannons, we must look behind the external, or the mask, to find reality. Throughout the play, we are asked to look "within," and to understand the real motives behind the actions of the characters.

The voice of the old man singing the song, "Oh, Shenandoah," introduces the action of the play with a "hopeless sea longing," which establishes the tragic mood of the entire trilogy. The singer, Seth, is the Mannon's handyman, and throughout the play he comments objectively upon people and events. He is accompanied by a group of townspeople who form a kind of Greek chorus through whose eyes we first see the Mannons.

Before we are introduced to the Mannon men, we are shown the women. It is at once apparent that mother and daughter are alike, but that the daughter resents the resemblance, and tries to make herself mannish and plain. This attempt to distinguish herself from her attractive mother is underlined by her rejection of her suitor, Peter, because she is needed at home by her father, and by her remark that she hates love.

After we learn that Adam Brant has been courting Lavinia and that Christine is also attracted to him, Seth calls attention to the likeness between Brant and all the Mannon men. They all wear a single "mask," just as do Christine, Lavinia and Adam's mother, Marie Brantôme. Lavinia asserts that she is like her father, but her face belies her words. It is Brant who first mentions the Blessed Isles in the South Seas, where people love without thinking of sin, and life is simple and conscienceless. Throughout the play, reference to the islands stands for a mother-fixation, a longing to return to the security of the mother. Brant, like the other Mannon men, tries to love his mother over again in other women. His revelation of his mother's suffering and his own desire for vengeance serves to introduce a central theme of the play: the lover-like relationship between mother and son.

ACT II

Soon after Christine admits to Lavinia that she hates her husband, she also declares she would not have fallen in love with Brant if her son Orin had been with her. Clearly Orin and his mother have an unnaturally close and dependent relationship. Ezra Mannon and Lavinia were responsible for Orin's leaving his mother to go off to war, and his absence precipitated her desire for revenge. She has gotten even with Ezra and her daughter as well, for she believes Lavinia loved Brant and is suffering because Christine won him. Christine is aware that Lavinia has always tried to usurp her role, wanting to become Ezra's wife and Orin's mother. Lavinia feels just as strongly that Christine has stolen the love Lavinia herself should have had all her life. The two are open, deadly enemies.

Christine feels that the Mannons have her under their thumb. She recalls that her husband used to be a judge and that in his heart, he plays the role still. Now that Lavinia knows Christine's secret, she can blackmail her mother and run her life. Christine's ultimate violence is largely explained by her desperation at the corner into which Lavinia has backed her. Christine explicitly indicates that the crime she and Brant are plotting is a realistic, necessary measure. She does not romanticize life, and throughout the play, her direct approach to love contrasts with the guiltridden, artificial mask of love common to the Mannons.

ACT III

When Ezra Mannon appears, it is clear that he has the same repressed, deadened air that marks Lavinia. He reminds his daughter that she has been taught never to cry, when she shows emotion over his return from the Civil War. After Ezra's suffering in the war and his contact with death, he reaches out to Christine for life and love, while Lavinia tries to intrude between them. Though eager to win back the affection of Christine, Ezra is quick to show jealousy of Adam Brant's supposed attentions to Lavinia. Quickly, Lavinia reassures her father that he is the only man in her life. Other jealousies, deeper in the past, at once appear. Ezra tells Christine how he resented Orin's birth, and how displaced he felt, and how even Lavinia's love did not make up for the loss of Christine's. He talks of the Mannon obsession with death and how the war showed him the barrier between husband and wife that made their existence a living death. He realizes that the wall exists because, like all Mannons, he cannot express love.

ACT IV

Ezra understands now that Christine has offered him no more than her body, that she does not love him as a person. It is her attitude which has given him feelings of guilt over his "lust." Christine tells him that his lack of tenderness and warmth made her unable to love him. As soon as Ezra knows the truth about himself and Christine, he dies. The contact of a Mannon with a genuine woman inevitably results in death.

THE HUNTED. ACT I

The 'chorus,' or group of townfolk commenting on the action, is generally sympathetic to Christine after Ezra Mannon's funeral. Their sentiments contrast with our first view of the widow after her crime, for she is now haggard and feverish-looking. It is obvious that she is already being tortured by her guilt, that she is one of the "haunted" of the title. She is primarily concerned with Orin's arrival, and worries that he will think she has lost her looks. Her concern on this point reminds us of her attitude toward her newly-returned husband. Christine had no wish to be attractive for Ezra.

Orin's feeling toward his father is clear at once. He says he had always assumed that his father would live forever, that is, that he would never live to take his father's place. He justifies his lack of emotion over Ezra's death by saying that Ezra himself taught his son not to cry. Thus, Ezra Mannon' sought to force the Mannon mask on his children, inhibiting their ability to express love.

ACT II

Orin senses that his father's presence is still in the house, as if he were aware that his father's unavenged ghost was not at rest. It is possible that Orin senses that his mother, who is now Brant's mistress, still does not belong solely to her son. Christine does her best to lull Orin's suspicions by reforging her old bonds with him. She says Orin is not a Mannon, but part of her, and that the two share a secret world. Like Brant and Ezra, Orin thinks of Christine as one with the islands of their dreams. For Orin, the island *is* Christine, and he wants nothing more in life than possession of it. He loves her so fiercely that he declares he could forgive her his father's murder, but that he could never forgive her if she betrayed him with a love affair. Despite her warmth toward Orin, Christine sees that he has been changed by the war and that he is preoccupied with death. This means that he is no longer on her side, but allied with the Mannons against her.

ACT III

When Orin stands near his father's body, we are shown his strong resemblance to Ezra. Christine's fears are justified. Orin confesses to Lavinia that during the war he dreamed that he killed his father and himself. Unconsciously, he has always desired to kill his father, and in his dream he even punishes himself for the crime. He regards life in the war as an "island of peace," and sees that the tangled intrigues of the Mannon house are more deadly and tormenting than the battle-front. When he suspects his mother's guilt, he begins to think of her as his "lost island." Now his longing for his mother mingles with his longing for death, and from this point on he does not separate the two.

ACT IV

Brant has a foreknowledge of his own death. He is depressed by the sea chanty which sings of a man who hanged his mother. This theme reveals the guilt of all men toward women, particularly toward their mothers. Brant had abandoned his own mother, Marie Brantôme, to her death, and now Orin is about to kill him, thus sealing Christine's doom. On the point of death, Brant, like Orin at his father's bier, identifies the Blessed Isles (mother) with peace and forgetfulness (death). Orin's murderous fury is aroused to a fever pitch by the knowledge that it is Brant whom Christine wants to accompany to the Islands, and not himself. When he has killed Brant, he dimly senses that he has killed his father and himself. In this way he is identified with Brant, who has indeed gone to the Blessed Isles and won peace.

ACT V

When Lavinia returns with Orin to tell Christine of Brant's murder, she is the image of her father. She represents all the Mannon harshness, stiffness and justice, and has completely taken the place of her father. Orin is not yet drawn to her as he will be in the third play; he is still Christine's and even while he tells her savagely of his hatred for the murdered Brant, he begs her forgiveness. Orin still wants to take his mother away to the Islands, away from the influence of all others, including Lavinia. When Christine shoots herself, Orin's first thought is that he has murdered her, and that he wants to follow her into death.

THE HAUNTED. ACT I

The chorus of townspeople reveals that the Mannon house is still not at rest. It is now Christine's presence that haunts it and her ghost that justice must lay to rest. When Lavinia appears after her trip to the Islands, it is as though Christine's ghost had taken flesh. She is now her mother all over again, even dressed in green (to symbolize fertility and earthiness), like Christine always was. Orin, on the other hand, has become the image of his father. He is stiff and lifeless, and admits he is no longer his mother's, but a Mannon. The two children now recapitulate, or re-live, their parents' marriage and tragedy. Orin recognizes that by Christine's death Lavinia had been set free to become her mother, and to Peter, Lavinia says she was "dead" in the old days.

Orin reveals his jealousy of Lavinia's interest in other men, duplicating his father's emotions. He hates the Islands, for his puritan conscience would not let him enjoy them as did Lavinia (in her new identity as Christine). Lavinia tells Peter that he reminds her of the natives and that the islands taught her to love. She is now warmly attracted to all the elemental, life-giving forces and repelled by Orin who represents death and judgment.

ACT II

Orin is now thoroughly possessed by his fate and wants to drag Lavinia down with him, like the Mannons always destroy the women chained to them. He accuses her of betraying him like Christine did, first with the native and then with the ship's officer who looked like Adam Brant. Lavinia like Christine, has lost all her Mannon-like power over events, and Orin has assumed control.

ACT III

When Lavinia prays for help in dealing with Orin, it is to the portraits of the Mannon ancestors. Like all the Mannons, she too is bound to the past and to the dead. Orin senses this too when he sees to it that she will be "punished" because she is a Mannon and should not escape the Mannon fate. He turns completely away from Hazel, who loves him, and tries to possess his sister as a lover. More and more he sees her, and desires her, as Christine, not herself, and he is desperate to bind her irrevocably to him. When Lavinia refuses his offer of love, Orin is bound to seek his mother in death. As he does so, Lavinia pours out to Peter her longing for love, for a simplified, unshadowed life. But when Orin is dead, Lavinia at once loses her identification with Christine and assumes the old stiff Mannon attitude.

ACT IV

Lavinia is determined to find happiness with Peter despite her fate, but she soon sees the folly of this. Already Peter has become uneasy and suspicious; she has contaminated his simple purity, just as the Mannons always do to those they love. Even while Lavinia embraces Peter, her thoughts dwell on death, and she sees that she is hopelessly bound to the Mannons. She acts as her own judge and punishes herself by sending Peter away and condemning herself to life in the dark, haunted Mannon house. Lavinia, too, recognizes that the Mannons must be punished simply "for being born." In the world of *Mourning Becomes Electra*, death is the punishment for life, a punishment which makes tragic the fate of every individual.

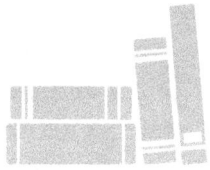

MOURNING BECOMES ELECTRA

ESSAY QUESTIONS AND ANSWERS

1. How is guilt to be understood in *Mourning Becomes Electra*? Of what sins are the main characters guilty?

The main burden of guilt in the play is borne by the male characters, despite the fact that Christine and Lavinia are more directly responsible for violence and death. Guilt is inevitably bound up with being born a man, for men grow up to be fathers. Fathers inevitably commit crimes against the woman, both wife and mother. Men are by nature clumsy in expressing love, while women are, in themselves, love's living expression. The men in the play regard women as goddesses, possessing the secret of happiness and peace, which can only be won by a man (he thinks) if he possesses the woman. Yet in possessing a woman, they kill her capacity for love, and for this 'murder' they must be punished. Their guilt is due to treason against the life-giving, love-affirming force represented by the female.

The older men in the Mannon family are all guilty of loving Marie Brantôme, Adam Brant's mother, selfishly and destructively. Ezra Mannon is guilty of letting Marie die unaided, and he repeats this crime when he kills Christine's love for him during their marriage. Lavinia, while she is still part of the father force and not a woman herself, is guilty of helping Ezra tear Orin from his mother to go to war. The mother is left bereaved and alone, through the fault of others, and she is not to be judged harshly for taking another "son-lover" in her desperate need. Orin wishes to be faithful to all that his mother represents, but his male, Mannon heritage, plus the masculine heritage of war, overcomes him. He is guilty, like the other Mannon men, of desiring to possess and thus to destroy the mother and love itself. He resents Lavinia's effort to love and live fully, just as he did Christine's. His guilt lies in his rejection of love and embrace of death.

2. What does the House represent to the people of the play?

The house is entirely a Mannon symbol. Christine hates it, and the father-dominated Lavinia loves it. The house represents the Mannon's guilt, for it was built by Abe Mannon after he had destroyed the old one. The old house had to be destroyed because the love of Marie Brantôme and David Mannon had defiled it. Thus, the new house, with its masklike front, is the symbol of the strict moral code of Abraham, Ezra and Orin Mannon.

People go to the Mannon house to die. Ezra is not killed at war, but in his bedroom. Christine runs into the house to shoot herself. Orin kills himself within its walls. Lavinia enters the house for a lifetime of lonely self-punishment. The rigorous, repressive Mannon conscience, which is the puritan code incarnate, *is* the house itself and acts as judge upon the characters.

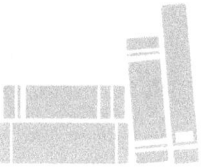

AH, WILDERNESS!

INTRODUCTION

During a protracted struggle with the writing of *Days Without End*, O'Neill decided to take a brief holiday. Overnight the characters and plot of *Ah, Wilderness!* came to him. He set to work and within a month, the first draft of the play was finished. He intended "to write a play true to the spirit of the American large small-town at the turn of the century." For the playwright, *Ah, Wilderness!* was "a dream walking," the resurrection of a dead past in American history before the urban, industrial age. He felt that the real America "found its unique expression in such middle-class families as the Millers."

Though O'Neill had intended the role of Richard to be the starring one, that of the father, Nat Miller, was considered principal. The first Nat Miller, George M. Cohan, thought little of the play's humor and saw it as stale vaudeville. Nevertheless, *Ah, Wilderness!*, which opened in 1933 with favorable reviews, ran two hundred and eighty-nine performances and earned for O'Neill about $75,000. Audiences often thought O'Neill was picturing his own youth in the play, but this was not all the case. *Long Day's Journey Into Night* far more accurately represented the tragic, rootless youngmanhood of the playwright. Of the happy family life in *Ah, Wilderness!*, O'Neill said he had only been "wishing out loud."

Yet there are aspects of the play that reflect O'Neill's past. Richard, Nat Miller's scholarly son, is sensitive, romantic and a lover of drama and poetry. Such traits were adapted for tragedy in *Long Day's Journey*, but in *Ah, Wilderness!*, they were distinctly comic. As a middle-aged man, the playwright viewed the solemn, radical poses of his youth with gentle mockery and understanding. He could tolerate the commonplace drabness and practicality of middle-class life and even see a certain beauty in it. *Ah, Wilderness!* shares the orthodox moral attitudes of *Days Without End*, but not its explicit piety. It stands in marked contrast to *The Iceman Cometh* and *Long Day's Journey Into Night*, the two utterly pessimistic plays that were to follow.

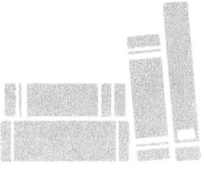

AH, WILDERNESS!

CHARACTER ANALYSIS

NAT MILLER

Miller is a tall, spare man in his fifties, who cares little about what he wears and what others think of him. He is a man of integrity, humor and generosity. Though mild-tempered, he can be roused to wrath, as his encounter with McComber proved. After his loss of temper on that occasion, Miller admits frankly that he sank to McComber's own level instead of sticking to his own principles. But his fault is due to his defense of Richard, in whose honesty Miller has great faith. He mentions Richard's innocence, and his own speech on associating with low women reveals that he shares this quality with his son.

ESSIE MILLER

Once a pretty, plump girl evidently much like Muriel is now, Essie is bustling, maternal and stout. She spends most of her time preparing meals and rebuking her children in a good-natured, automatic way, whenever they offend against her code of "good manners." She does not understand Richard and disapproves of his dangerous reading, but she is proud of his giftedness.

SID DAVIS

Short and stout like his older sister Essie, Sid is a clownish, child-like man who is irresponsible to an extreme. He cannot keep promises or jobs, but his light-hearted attitude toward life causes everyone to warm to him.

LILY MILLER

An old maid school teacher type, Lily is tall and thin like her brother Nat. Though she is gentle and kind, Lily has a rigid, perfectionist view of life that contrasts with Miller's tolerant, out-going one.

ARTHUR MILLER

Arthur is big and tough, a football player who conforms with delight to the collegiate stereotype. He is concerned to be fashionable and to squire the right girl to the right social event. Clearly, he is more Essie's son than Nat's.

RICHARD MILLER

Richard is a perfect blend of both his parents, harmonizing their good qualities. Because of his adolescent phase, he is alternately a tempestuous, idealistic boy and a self-conscious poser.

MURIEL MCCOMBER

Muriel is a blend of practicality and frivolity. She obeys her father in writing the letter to Richard, but leaves the house behind his back. Richard cannot understand her lack of integrity, but her simplicity, beauty and purity charm him. Like Essie, she wants Richard to go to Yale and be respectable and does not understand his transition to manhood.

AH, WILDERNESS!

SUMMARY

ACT I

From the beginning of the play, Richard appears to be at a time of crisis and transition. He is reliving the adolescent rebellion and sense of tragic self-awareness that Miller so vividly remembers in his own past. We see, through Richard, what Miller was like as a young man. Through Miller, we see the man Richard will someday be. The seasoned maturity of Miller contrasts with the turbulent, youthful emotion of Richard. Instead of O'Neill's usual harsh, cold father image, the character of Nat Miller is both sensitive and understanding. Youth in this play is not a period of horror, but a transition to manhood marked by tolerance and nobility. The normal attitude of Miller and his wife toward sex and drinking contrasts with the puritanical, sterile attitude of Lily. It is clear that the children will have the accepting, warm feeling toward life that their parents do, and that they will not wind up like Lily and Mr. McComber.

ACT II

Richard assumes the pose of a violent pessimist. He has become a rebel against established order and authority on the symbolic day, July 4th. When his Aunt Lily is shocked at his cynicism, he says women are only concerned with what is "nice." Now, as a man, Richard declares himself ready to "face life." Essie laughs at him openly, refusing to admit he is not her baby any longer, but Miller understands his son's rebellion and treats him with respect. As if to mark Richard's coming of age, Miller involuntarily reveals his own passage out of the prime of life. He is caught by the family telling old, oft repeated stories and is ashamed of his lapse of memory.

ACT III

In this act, Richard encounters a sordid aspect of love which shocks his romantic sensibilities. Belle is not an idealized prostitute like Anna Christie, nor is her influence long-lasting, as was that of Marsden's prostitute in *Strange Interlude*. Belle is callous, greedy and totally uninterested in Richard's suggestion that she reform. Her attitude toward Richard stands in strong dramatic contrast to that of Essie in the following scene and of Muriel in the following act.

ACT IV

While waiting for Muriel, Richard thinks of Belle and his consequent thoughts of Muriel are briefly sensual because of his experience the night before. He struggles to maintain his purity and succeeds, just as his father did before him. The night after he came home drunk with liquor, Richard comes home drunk again, but this time with love. For the first time he is able to see his father as a human being like himself, who loves and is loved. Miller observes that Richard has made a stride forward, symbolized by the loving kiss the son gives the father. He sees that his son is now "safe from himself," and that life can do nothing to him that he cannot deal with life a man. The transition that Richard has made is one that makes him a man. He is now able to love and to weather love's disappointment, and he knows that drink and low women cannot serve him as an avenue of escape when life is hard.

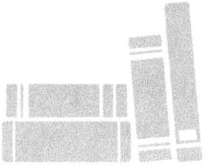

AH, WILDERNESS!

ESSAY QUESTIONS AND ANSWERS

....

Question: What issues in the lives of the Millers are resolved and what issues remain to be dealt with at the end of the play?

Answer: The one issue that is truly resolved in the play is Richard's coming of age. He achieves a new closeness and understanding with his father, and this occurs because he has combatted his first great temptation. The incident has cast him permanently is the same mold of manhood that formed his father.

No one else in the play can be said to resolve any issues that affect his life. Sid continues to propose to Lily, but they go on together as before, without hope of marriage. Essie cannot be said to come to any real understanding of Miller or Richard, but she loves them and that is sufficient. Richard's romance is left dangling. Miller realizes that Muriel may become fat and no longer be the figure of romance in Richard's eyes that she now is. Essie suggests, practically, that Muriel will be forgotten when Richard is away at college, but Miller says he hopes Richard will not ever forget this first romance. Thus, events in the play serve mainly to reveal character and not to resolve a plot. Miller sees that all these things go to make up a past that may be reflected upon and learned from, and in this lies their value and meaning.

Question: How are the two generations linked in the play?

Answer: The bond of love reveals most clearly the resemblance between the young and the middle-aged in *Ah, Wilderness!*. Miller, at the end of the play, sees himself and Essie as "surrounded by love." Through the romances of their children, the love of the Millers is extended and enriched. Their marriage represents fulfillment and fertility in the play, while the hopeless courting of Lily by Sid David represents a love that is too weak for responsibility and productiveness. Wint Selby, like Sid Davis, is a man who plays at love for his own selfish pleasure, and his attitude is specifically rejected by Richard as part of his new manhood. Richard binds himself permanently to his father and his father's ideals when he imitates his father's attitude toward love. He even chooses a woman like his mother, pretty, plump and practical, about whom he weaves his fantasies and romantic poetry. As Richard becomes a man and experiences real love, the two generations blend into one; he joins his father in maturity.

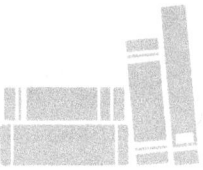

THE ICEMAN COMETH

INTRODUCTION

In spite of production difficulties, *The Iceman Cometh* opened October 9, 1946, with an advance ticket sale of $262,000. Reporters from all over the world were assigned to the opening. During the winter of 1946-47, O'Neill and his wife Carlotta were much sought out and feted by fashionable and artistic circles, but they did not enjoy being lionized. More and more, O'Neill felt at ease only among his old friends. Both in his personal life and in his plays he returned to the past. He told one writer: "I do not think you can write anything of value or understanding about the present. You can only write about life if it is far enough in the past." Like the characters in *Long Day's Journey Into Night* and *The Iceman Cometh*, O'Neill saw the present in terms of the dramatic reality of the past.

The World War and his own tragic personal affairs had made O'Neill deeply pessimistic about the nature and future of man. About the time Iceman was written, he was asked what he felt about the destiny of mankind in view of the agony of its present. O'Neill replied, "It will take a man a million years to grow up and obtain a soul." He indicated to the cast of the play that he felt revenge motivated men's behavior, and that the characters of the play should be revealed as weak, not simply evil. Because there had been an indication in plays written just before Iceman that O'Neill had a resurgence of religious faith, he was asked if he had returned to the Catholic Church. "Unfortunately no," he replied, "The Iceman is a denial of any other experience of faith in my plays. In writing it, I felt I had locked myself in with my memories." Evidently, O'Neill meant the play to reflect the pessimism and nihilism that had come to dominate his mind and heart by the end of his life.

The characters of *The Iceman Cometh* resemble those of *The Hairy Ape*: they do not "belong." They do not seek happiness, honor, love or money, merely peace. In the play, there are three ways to win peace: drink, pipe, dream (illusion), or death. The characters had all come to a tragic end before the play's beginning; all were failures who could not cope with reality, except Hickey. Hickey offers to the group at the saloon a way out of their hopeless existence that will free them of the pipe dreams of guilt, hope or personal reform. He tells them that the real answer to the riddle of life's meaning is that there is no answer. Larry Slade has already put much of Hickey's philosophy into action, but he cannot bring himself to embrace death. He has cut himself loose from all values, hope and close human contacts, vainly hoping that a man can exist in a void or limbo. This pipe dream is blasted like all the others in the play, and Parritt's suicide leaves Larry with a vision of life's complete futility.

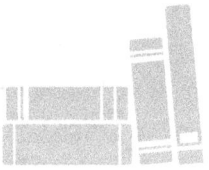

THE ICEMAN COMETH

CHARACTER ANALYSIS

LARRY SLADE

A gaunt, slovenly Irishman, Larry has the contrasting features of a mystic's blue, piercing eyes and a sardonically humorous manner. He is sixty years old, and trying to overcome a craven fear of death which he refuses to admit. He left the Syndicalist-Anarchist movement as a young man, because he could not bear the constant betrayals of his mistress, the free-thinking Rosa Parritt. He has become convinced that men are too vile to cooperate in building a new society. Ever since he left the movement, he has tried to cut himself off from life and other people, observing them bitterly and mockingly from a "grandstand." Because of his innate compassion, however, he cannot help being sucked back into the mainstream of life.

HARRY HOPE

Harry is a thin, temperamental old man, who puts on a belligerent manner only to hide his sentimental softness and affection for all those who are parasites on him. Twenty years before, he lost his tyrannical wife, Bessie, who had propelled him up the ladder toward a minor political post. Since her death, he has remained in his saloon, afraid to immerse himself in real life, content with drink and the companions which his charity has bound to him.

THEODORE HICKMAN (HICKEY)

Hickey is a plump, bald man of fifty, with a salesman's smile, good humor and shrewdness about people and their unconscious desires. He is the son of a midwestern evangelist, but he early became the town bad boy. Despite his reputation, Evelyn, a girl of noble character and good family, loved him and insisted on marrying him. She continued to forgive him and love him no matter how many times he was unfaithful to her and got drunk. Hickey pretended to himself that he really loved her and killed her only to avoid disappointing her again. His real feeling, however, is hatred, and a conviction that she humiliated him by her righteousness and forgiveness. He is sure that now all his illusions are gone and he is a free man and wants to sell this "religion" to all his old friends so he will no longer be alone.

DON PARRITT

Parritt is a thin, blond eighteen-year-old, who dresses flashily and cannot help revealing an unpleasant, defiant attitude. Though he cannot admit it to himself until the end of the play, Parritt hated his mother for being a loose woman: he was jealous of her lovers and felt they robbed him of the real home he deserved. He tries to pretend he sold his mother and the Movement out for money or for love of a prostitute girl-friend, but his real motive tortures him, causing him to long for punishment.

PAT MCGLOIN

An old, ex-policeman, McGloin is still bitter about being caught at graft. He dreams of being re-instated so he can chisel some more, like all his ex-colleagues do.

JAMES CAMERON (JIMMY TOMORROW)

Jimmy is a prim, gentle, little man, dressed neatly in black. He is a man of some intelligence and education, but has a little-boy air of irresponsibility and guilelessness about him. He is sure that just for the asking he can get his old publicity job back, from which he was sacked for drunkenness. He continually tells himself that all he needs to do is make a good appearance and his life will change.

WILLIE OBAN

The son of a wealthy criminal who wound up in jail, Willie cannot forget the humiliations of his past. He was a brilliant law student at Harvard and dreams vainly of returning to the bar. His father had tried to run Willie's life, but Willie had escaped through drink. Now, in his thirties, Willie is thin and dissipated, in the last stages of alcoholism. His mother has disowned him and will give him no more handouts.

THE ICEMAN COMETH

SUMMARY

ACT I

The name of the saloon where the wretched group has gathered, "Harry's Hope's," is ironic, for each one of his guests is hopeless. However, all of them continue to hope, and they put their faith in "pipe dreams." Larry, the objective commentator on the action, tells us in the beginning that "truth has no bearing on anything," and that only pipe dreams sustain men. He also realizes that the group is happy in its own way.

Rocky declares that the saloon is like a morgue because all the men have passed out, and he longs for Hickey's coming which will bring life to the place. He mentions Hickey's obsessive joke about finding his virtuous wife "in bed with the iceman." This is our first introduction to a **theme** that runs throughout the play: Hickey is, ironically, a bringer of death, an "iceman."

Larry reveals that he cannot help pitying Willie Oban, despite his own decision that he will only observe life and not involve himself in it. Parritt's appearance begins a conflict that is not resolved until the play's end, when Parritt kills himself and Larry is reconciled to death. Parritt and Hickey are, in a sense, part of Larry, and their fate influences his. It is through Parritt that Larry learns he cannot avoid taking responsibility in life, and through Hickey he learns how to banish his last pipe dream: the fear of death. Death is not to be feared when the worthlessness of life is clearly revealed.

ACT II

The coming of Hickey results in disquietude and quarreling among all the members of the group. The death of the pipe dream means the death of hope and happiness. This causes men to turn against each other in sullen fury. Larry tells the anarchist Hugo that Hickey's new Movement is one "that'll blow up the world." The little world of the saloon is already on the verge of chaos because of the "iceman". Larry pities the poor souls who are losing their dreams, but Hickey declares that Larry's pity is a false and destructive one. Peace can never be found until reality is faced.

Hickey sees that he, Parritt and Larry are linked together and that they have all suffered because of a woman. Parritt was bound to his mother and Hickey to his wife. Both felt devoured by their women and both felt compelled to destroy them. Larry, on the other hand, refused to stay with a woman who did not belong to him alone, yet this refusal did not free him from involvement with her and her son.

ACT III

The ruptures between old friends become more severe as each goes out to seek his new life. The implication is that friendship cannot continue when people are engaged in an active pursuit of the good life for themselves. The group can only maintain itself without conflict if all its members are at the bottom of the heap and doing nothing to better themselves. Larry and Harry see the essential inhumanity of Hickey's evangelistic crusade on behalf of reality. They realize that it can only torment men and lead them to suicide. Hickey reveals that he expects the efforts of the men to fail; only when they see that all effort and hope are futile, will they achieve peace. The peace is that of death. When Harry returns, shaken, from his attempt to leave the saloon, everyone agrees he looks "dead."

ACT IV

Parritt identifies himself completely with Larry, and suggests that Larry is actually the one contemplating a jump from the fire escape because of disappointed love. Larry senses that in acting as Parritt's executioner, he is also being his own. He cannot face death freely until he has "executed" Parritt first.

Hickey becomes resentful and baffled when he learns that no one else has found peace by his recommended method. This drives him to confess his crime, and ultimately, to fall victim to a pipe dream himself. He admits involuntarily that he hated his wife for being so righteous and that he killed out of hate, not love. Then, because he cannot live without his pipe dream, Hickey decides he must have been insane when he committed the murder.

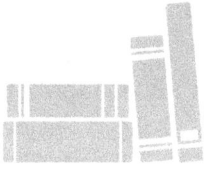

THE ICEMAN COMETH

ESSAY QUESTIONS AND ANSWERS

Question: How is the relationship of love to hate revealed in the actions of the play's central characters, and in their attitudes?

Answer: *The Iceman Cometh* indicates that the hopelessness of society is largely due to man's inability to love without that love's turning into hate. As long as the characters merely "dream" about action, they are able to love each other. When they attempt to act in the real world, that love becomes hate. Men resent being bound to other men; they resent responsibility. Therefore, they lash out against one another for revenge.

Because he loved Rosa Parritt, Larry suffered, and his love turned to hate, though he will not admit this. He revealed his hatred by leaving the Movement, which meant more to Rosa than anything in the world. Parritt likewise expressed his hatred of all that bound him to the mother whom he also loved. His betrayal was an act of hatred that was a reaction against love. Hickey's hatred of his wife was born out of their mutual love and the restraints it put on his freedom. The central **theme** of the play is not love, but death, into which love has been changed.

Question: What dramatic and symbolic functions do Hickey and Parritt serve in the play?

Answer: Hickey is an outsider, in the world of Hope's saloon. Like Parritt, he is destined to bring changes into a static situation. He is a representation of the real world, the business world outside the saloon, just as Parritt represents violent political involvement. As invaders from reality they destroy the peace of illusion that has existed at Harry Hope's. Hickey has stopped drinking in marked contrast to the members of the saloon group. This is a symbol for his fatal clarity of vision, just as liquor is a symbol for the dream life of the derelicts. Hickey and Parritt also serve to bring about Larry's final moral crisis. Parritt demands action and commitment from Larry; he will not accept the excuse that Larry has withdrawn from life. Hickey forces Larry to face the ultimate reality of death as the price for involvement in existence. Larry's philosophical problems are thus dramatized in the persons of two vivid characters instead of being merely talked about in monologue or dialogue.

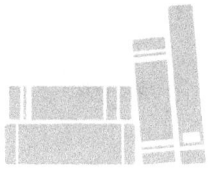

LONG DAY'S JOURNEY INTO NIGHT

INTRODUCTION

Eugene O'Neill finished *Long Day's Journey Into Night* in 1941. When he sent it to his New York editor, he ordered that the play was not to be produced or published until twenty-five years after he was dead. The play reveals many sordid facts about the O'Neill family that O'Neill felt were best left unknown while those living could be affected by the publicity. The principal objector to the publication of the play was Eugene O'Neill, Jr., the son of his first marriage and a brilliant young professor of classics at Yale University. When his son committed suicide, O'Neill changed his mind about the play and told his wife Carlotta that the time limit need not be observed. Carlotta O'Neill has said that her husband wept as he wrote this play, a bitter and tragic reminiscence of his childhood and young manhood. Despite its lack of plot and its long quotations of poetry, the play has been rated one of O'Neill's greatest and most moving dramas.

When O'Neill was dead, Carlotta invited the great director José Quintero, who had put on *The Iceman Cometh*, to take charge of the production of *Long Day's Journey Into Night*. Quintero looked upon this commission as a great honor, and even a "sacred charge." His sensitive production of the play started an O'Neill revival and won O'Neill his fourth Pulitzer Prize.

Though *Long Day's Journey Into Night* lacks a plot, in the conventional sense, it is not therefore less dramatic than his other works. Whatever plot there is in the play is not confined to the single day of the dramatic action, but reaches far into the past of the Tyrone family. We see the drama of the past reflected in the suffering of the present, for the latter is entirely an outgrowth of the former. The day of the action is a day of crisis for the family, during which the past is relived and the future clearly outlined. The mother resumes her drug habit on the same day that the youngest son learns he has tuberculosis. The play does not have a climax, but is itself the climax in the story of the Tyrone (O'Neill) family.

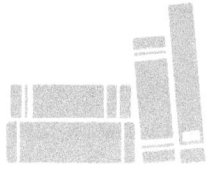

LONG DAY'S JOURNEY INTO NIGHT

CHARACTER ANALYSIS

JAMES TYRONE:

A strong, handsome man, Tyrone looks younger than his sixty-five years. His bearing is graceful and almost military in character; in this as in his gestures, he reflects his actor's profession. Tyrone's voice is resonant and flexible, and a matter of great pride to him. He is a healthy, stolid man whose lack of nerves reflects his Irish peasant ancestry. Occasionally he shows signs of sensitivity and pride in his art, but for the most part, his simple background has made him crassly materialistic.

MARY TYRONE:

Though she is fifty-four and her face is pale from illness, Mary Tyrone has kept her striking prettiness. She is very nervous; her fingers, knotted by arthritis, drum constantly on the table. Whenever she feels that someone is looking at her, Mary nervously re-arranges her hair. She can never forget that she was once a great beauty, and feels it necessary to be thought pretty by those she loves. The charm and innocence of her school days in the convent are still upon her, but these contrast sadly with the bitterness and cynicism to which she occasionally gives vent when the pressures of life grow too much for her.

JAMES TYRONE, JR.:

In face and form, Jamie resembles his father, but he does not have the actor's grace and handsomeness. Though his mouth is perpetually cynical and sneering, he also possesses a certain Irish charm and whimsical sense of humor. Jamie is devoted to his mother and totally at odds with his father. By his lazy life, he protests against his father's main trait: his miserliness. Jamie rebels against all his father stands for. He mocks the search for security, respectability and conventional morality. Because he is a failure in life at the age of thirty-three, he is jealous of Edmund's small successes. Even though he genuinely loves his younger brother, Jamie cannot help feeling hostile to him because it was Edmund's birth that started their mother on drugs. By tempting Edmund to lead a dissolute life, he is able to revenge himself on his father and mother, as well as to keep Edmund from succeeding where he himself has failed.

EDMUND TYRONE:

Edmund is ten years younger than his brother. He resembles both his parents, particularly Mary. Both mother and son have high foreheads, large poetic eyes, and nervous, sensitive hands. They share a high-strung temperament, and they are both ill, the mother with arthritis and the son with tuberculosis. Not having had as much experience with his mother's drug addiction as Jamie, Edmund is more optimistic. When she slips back into the habit, Edmund's sorrow and disillusionment are even more profound than Jamie's. At this point in his life, he begins to seek out his father, for the first time understanding him as a human being with guilt, suffering and disappointments of his own. Throughout the day of the play's action, young Edmund is clearly in the process of growing up. He comes to terms with his past, with both parents' failures and with Jamie's real attitude toward him. The others are clearly doomed, but Edmund is young, he has published a little poetry, and he is going away to a sanatorium, hopefully to be cured. He is the one figure in the play that is not completely tragic.

Comment

ACT I

Within the first few moments of the play, we are introduced to the weaknesses of each member of the family. At first, these weaknesses are only lightly mentioned by the characters. But as the play goes on they are returned to again and again. More sordid details and more bitterness are revealed, until at last all the feelings of the family are out in the open.

Throughout the play, the foghorn introduces a note of reality. It causes lack of sleep and a remembrance of tragic events in the present and the past. The fog lifts itself, present throughout the action of the play, represents the hopeless atmosphere in which the characters must function. They do not know where they have come from, why they are here or what they may hope from the future. All they know is suffering; it has formed their lives and their feelings about one another.

Tyrone and his oldest son, Jamie, despite their hostility, have one bond: their common love for Mary. They both flatter her about her looks, and she is eager to look pretty for Jamie as well as for her husband. Part of Jamie's jealousy of Edmund clearly stems from his knowledge that Edmund's birth brought about their mother's gray hair, physical weakness and drug addiction.

ACT II

When Mary appears in a drugged state, she reveals a clear awareness of reality, except for her own addiction. This failing she will not admit. But she feels free to comment objectively and forcefully on the failings of others. One moment she excuses faults by relating them to tragedies of the past; the next moment she criticizes the offender even more severely. Whenever she blames anyone, including herself, she always returns to a detached attitude of forgiveness, saying "he can't help being what the past has made him." Mary is always looking for her glasses, which symbolize clarity of spiritual vision. She wants her lost religious faith back and her lost childhood happiness.

Her suffering, Mary believes, is due to God's punishment of her sins: negligence in the case of the baby's death, and loss of faith in Him. While she admits these sins, she does not want to admit her dope addiction, just as she does not want to admit that Edmund is really ill with tuberculosis. Both illnesses frighten her too much for her to face them. She feels that by her neglect of little Eugene, she proved she did not deserve to have Edmund. If Edmund is sick, it is a case of God's punishing her again. Mary declares to Edmund that she has lost her soul, and will only be whole again when her men lead good lives and she can stop feeling guilty.

ACT III

When Mary talks to Cathleen about the fog and the past, their parallel monologues represent the confrontation of reality and illusion. While Mary remarks dreamily about the effect the drug is having on her, Cathleen discusses the pinches of the chauffeur and the notion that the fog is good for the complexion. Cathleen's cheerfully admiring attitude toward the Tyrone marriage and the life of an actor contrasts strongly with Mary's expression of her emptiness and loneliness. One of Mary's main complaints comes to light because of the inhibitions removed by the drug: her father had balked at no expense when it came to Mary, and Tyrone was exactly the opposite. Like many O'Neill characters, Mary is a victim of a close bond to a parent which interferes with a normal relationship to the husband.

ACT IV

Edmund says to his father, "Who wants to see life as it is, if they can help it?" This line expresses one of the dominant themes in the play. Each character has his own method of escape: Mary has her drugs, Tyrone and Jamie their liquor, and Edmund has his poetic sense of personal dissolution in nature and death. Like the characters of *The Iceman Cometh*, all the Tyrones see life as a tragic affair, during which people try in one way or another to avoid confronting the tragedy.

By the end of the last act Jamie has begun to disintegrate. He admits his jealousy and the fact that he has tried to drag

Edmund as low as himself. From this point on, Edmund rises to a position of dominance, to the position of "older brother." This even is the climax of the play, if the play can be said to have a climax. It confirms Edmund as the family's only hope. What Jamie has always feared has happened: the pet of the family has displaced him, despite all that he could do to prevent it.

LONG DAY'S JOURNEY INTO NIGHT

ESSAY QUESTIONS AND ANSWERS

1. What dramatic devices does O'Neill use to reveal the past in *Long Day's Journey Into Night*?

The quarrel is the primary technique O'Neill uses to reveal the past to the audience. Since the Tyrone family is a family of actors, the quarrels become highly dramatic affairs, with much emotion and highly charged language poured into each one. Almost invariably, after the quarrel has served its purpose and made clear one more event in the Tyrone past, there are quick apologies and reconciliations. The quarrel thus serves ti make evident the underlying affection of the characters for each other despite their bitterness at the wrongs that have been done.

Mary's dope addiction and the men's drunkenness are also devices for relaying information about the past. With the removal of inhibitions, the characters can speak freely to one another about their real motivations and resentments. Instead of using the "aside" technique as he did in *Strange Interlude*, O'Neill could let his characters speak freely to one another, all the barriers having been broken down by drugs and alcohol.

2. How does each of the characters finally come to regard "reality" in the play?

Throughout *Long Day's Journey Into Night*, reality is a source of suffering, and almost never a source of joy. The sound of the foghorn, which recalls the characters to the reality of the present, is considered a frightening and unpleasant sound. Over and over again, through the observations and remembrances of the characters, we are shown past realities that explain their tragic and hopeless attitudes.

Edmund suggests in the last act that no one really wants to see unrelieved reality. When Edmund talks about his desire for death, he is openly saying what the rest of the characters only hint at: it is better to die than to exist in the real world as they know it. All the characters seek consolation for past ills and oblivion for the present and the future. Despite the fact that the past is occasionally looked on with nostalgia, it is apparent that the ugly realities of the past have conditioned the hopeless realities of the present.

A TOUCH OF THE POET

INTRODUCTION

A Touch of the Poet was the third play in a projected cycle of plays that was to deal with the history of America. It was the only play of the cycle to be either published or produced. Yale University published the text of the play in 1957 and it was produced in New York on October 2 the following year. One critic has called the cycle "probably the most stupendous task ever undertaken by a modern playwright." The overall title of the cycle was *A Tale of the Possessors Self-Dispossessed* and its central **theme** was to have been the corruption of character through materialistic greed, a central point in O'Neill's mature philosophy. In *A Touch of the Poet*, however, it is not so much greed that determines the fate of the characters as it is the past. Each of the characters is pictured fighting his own past, his family background. Ultimately no one escapes the accumulated force of tradition, although in this particular play the result is not tragedy.

In *A Touch of the Poet*, O'Neill dramatized the contact between a family of impetuous Irishmen with the more staid New England Yankee society of the early nineteenth century. As in *Mourning Becomes Electra*, the straitjacket morality of puritan New England is shown to be sterile and essentially dead. It is implied that the old puritan stock will be transformed and given new life by the more earthy and passionate Irishmen who will marry into the Yankee families. The play is the story of Major Cornelius Melody, a tavernkeeper who lives outside of Boston and has pretensions to gentility. His daughter, Sara, falls in love with a Harvard boy. Their love serves as a bridge between the world of the Irish immigrant and that of the stuffy, morality-minded puritan elite. It was O'Neill's intention in the next play of the cycle to show how both families are reborn through their love. The play was never written, although O'Neill may have finished a rough draft of it. Shortly before he died he burned a number of manuscripts he knew he would never be able to complete.

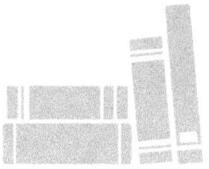

A TOUCH OF THE POET

CHARACTER ANALYSIS

MAJOR CORNELIUS MELODY

Major Melody is a man's man. He loves to drink, hunt and chase women. He is a braggart and takes great delight in boasting of his exploits in war and with women. His code is that of the passionate man. What he does he does to excess or not at all. He is intensely proud and is in his best good humor when he has a sympathetic audience that will listen to his tales and relish them. He does not have the means, however, to support his pretensions, and runs himself into debt to keep the mare that is the symbol of his pride. He scorns the Yankee gentlemen of Boston because to him they are effeminate, neither able to fight or make love with gusto. He also scorns religion, because it would limit the expression of his masculine spirit, which is itself a kind of religion to him. When he no longer believes in himself as the great man for whom all things are possible, he becomes another man, a peasant who has neither the capacity nor the desire to live above the level of mere animal existence.

NORA MELODY

Overwork and worry have made Nora appear much older than her forty years. Although slovenly in appearance, she still retains some of her former beauty. She is sweet and simple and wants nothing more than to please her husband, for whom she is constantly making excuses to her daughter. Like Melody she is a passionate person, and it is her pride in her love that has sustained her. She is proud that she gave herself to her husband completely, and did not allow her religion to place conditions on her love. She has moments when she wonders whether she did the right thing in giving herself utterly to Melody, but she dismisses such thoughts and will not allow them to trouble her. Her heart is broken when she sees her husband degenerate from a dashing soldier with aristocratic manners to a leering and fawning peasant.

SARA MELODY

Sara has seen what a demanding life her mother has led and has determined never to give herself completely to any man, lest he scorn and reject her after he has power over her. She wants reason to control her life and thinks that if she uses her head she can manage her life so she will have all the advantages her mother never had. In spite of her resolve to control her life, Sara loses herself to Simon. Her love cannot be controlled and she ends by giving herself completely to her lover as her mother did before her. At the beginning of the play she does not understand why her mother tolerates her father, but by the end of the play she sympathizes with her mother and no longer hates her father. She has discovered the power of love.

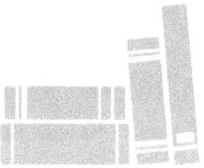

A TOUCH OF THE POET

SUMMARY

ACT I

In the first act the major tensions of the play are only suggested. Major Melody shows nothing of his peasant ancestry, but it is clear that both he and his tavern have seen better days. Nora is dressed in a slovenly fashion, and Sara, in spite of her youth and beauty, has in her appearance a touch of coarseness and sensuality. The physical appearance of the characters and the tavern suggests the tension that will be fully developed later in the play. They have the atmosphere of aristocracy that has fallen upon evil days, or the incomplete mingling of the aristocrat and the peasant. Sara's concern for money and her constant bickering with her father also indicate that the aristocratic from Melody puts up is a very weak facade, and that it will fall before the play is over.

ACT II

In the second act the underlying tensions of the play begin to make themselves known. Sara is warring with herself about

Simon. She does not want to give herself to him as her mother has given herself to Melody, but passion is sweeping her off her feet. Melody's pretensions to aristocracy suffer their first serious blow when Simon's mother refuses to let him kiss her. Success with women has always been one of the great buttresses of his pride, and when she refuses him his manhood is shaken.

ACT III

After his failure with Deborah, Melody flings himself into his celebration of the anniversary of the battle of Talavera. Through excessive drinking and the singing of hunting songs, activities that are specifically masculine, he attempts to bolster his weakening pride. His treatment of Nicholas Gadsby reflects his threatened manhood. He must have him thrown out to prove he is still a man's man. Nora reminds the audience of Sara's conflict between heart and head when she says that true love (passionate love) will not let anything stand in its way.

ACT IV

When Nora decides against confessing to a priest that she let Melody make love to her before their marriage, she reveals her tie to the past and to her love. Her decision is to remain true to love and deny the claim of what she thinks of as an abstract moral code. According to the values of the play this is a good decision, and she resolves her conflict successfully. Sara also resolves her conflict successfully in the moral terms suggested by the play. In committing herself completely to Simon she also decides in favor of the passionate life, which in the play is the only life worth living. When Melody is unsuccessful in his fight with Harford's servants and the police, the last shred of his manhood is taken from him. He has lost his touch with women, and has failed in personal combat. At this point he kills the mare which is the symbol of his aristocratic pretensions. He degenerates to his ancestral past in much of the same way that Brutus Jones does in *The Emperor Jones*. His wife and daughter would rather have the old Major with whom they are familiar, but that is impossible. Although his degeneration has tragic overtones, it is, nevertheless, in the context of the play, a natural process, and hence not evil in itself. What he degenerates to is a natural existence in which passion and pride will continue to operate, but on a lower level than they did when he was able to maintain his identity as an aristocrat.

BRIGHT NOTES STUDY GUIDE

A TOUCH OF THE POET

ESSAY QUESTIONS AND ANSWERS

Question: How are each of the main characters in the play haunted by the past? Is this always bad, or does some good come from it?

Answer: Major Melody tried to escape his peasant ancestry by adopting the manners of the aristocracy and living a gay, devil-may-care life. In doing so he was guilty of the sin of pride. He set himself up above the other Irish immigrants and lorded it over them. He made his wife's life miserable by treating her as if she were below him. He tells her to her face that she is a peasant, and humiliates her. However, his past catches up with him. His father had been a peasant and once the Major sees his own gallantry as silly and ineffectual, he reverts to his peasant ancestry.

Nora Melody cannot break away from her husband even though he treats her badly. When she let him make love to her before they were married, she gave herself to him body and soul, and she can never take back the gift of herself. It is through the continuous giving of herself that she is able to achieve the honor without which she could not live. By acquiescing in the demands of the past, which are for her demands of love, her life gains dignity.

Sara Melody would like to break away from the pattern set by her mother. She would like to rule her life by reason and common sense, because she sees how much her mother has suffered by living the law of the heart.

However, she is unable to escape the bonds of unqualified love. They constitute her inheritance from the past. She repeats with Simon the same sin her mother committed with Melody. Once she has sinned with Simon she gives up all to her love. Like her father, she must do to excess all that she does.

The play suggests that the man who tries to escape his past is guilty of the sin of pride. For the Major, Nora and Sara, the past means a following of the heart, a life of exuberant dedication to the impulses of the moment, come what may. Such a life is not always easy, but the play suggests it is always honorable, and certainly more human than adherence to an abstract code of morality would be. The play exalts passionate humanity as the highest goal of human life.

CONCLUSION

O'NEILL AND AMERICAN LITERATURE

When Eugene O'Neill began to write, American drama was limited to insipid melodrama and trivial comedy. It had never been considered part of American literature, as such. More than any other playwright O'Neill helped to create a serious American drama. He did so by remaining uncompromisingly himself. His goal was not the creation of a serious American drama, but rather the full expression of the truth he believed he had in him. Indeed, he felt that America had failed. One of the central **themes** of his incomplete cycle of plays dealing with American history was the destruction of people through greed.

THE MEN O'NEILL ADMIRED

The men O'Neill admired did not possess great wealth or high position in society. He had learned in his seafaring days to admire simple men who responded directly to the challenge of a hostile world. And in spite of what he considered the hostility of the world, O'Neill obviously took great delight in an adventurous life lived close to nature. Like Paddy of *The Hairy Ape*, he longed for the days of sailing ships. He did not feel at home in the modern world. Whenever one of the down-and-out friends of his youth appealed to him for aid, he responded with immediate generosity, much to the dismay of his third wife who felt he had risen above their company.

THE PROBLEM OF MODERN MAN

O'Neill was an autobiographical writer. He said he had never written anything he had not experienced either directly or indirectly. He was far more interested in the relationship of individuals with the world than with each other. The chief problem of modern man, as he saw it, was the death of the old, orthodox conception of God and the inability of science and materialism to provide a new one for the religious instinct that yet survived. The sea of faith had retreated, leaving man high and dry.

O'NEILL'S ANSWER

O'Neill's answer to this problem is not a happy one. Man is alone in the universe and yet he must not knuckle under. Above all he must continue to follow his dream, whatever that may be. He must keep himself free from the corrupting power of wealth and position. Above all he must not sell out to the easy life, but continue to strive for the unknowable, no matter what the cost.

HIS DRAMATIC IMAGINATION

O'Neill had a comprehensive imagination and a broad experience of life. The sheer scope and power of his plays overwhelm the audience. Like Dreiser, he was deficient as a literary stylist. He was not, in fact, a literary writer, nor would he have wanted to be thought one. Although capable of writing eloquent prose, there is little poetry of language in his plays. However, intensity of emotion, breadth of scope and originality of plot more than make up for the lack of poetry. The chief defect of his plays is their length, and he cut them readily right up to the day of production. It is likely that future performances of his major plays will be freely cut by directors.

HIS INFLUENCE

It is hard to determine O'Neill's influence on contemporary American drama. He demonstrated that important **themes** could be handled on the stage and would be respected by American audiences. And yet it is difficult to find individual playwrights who have been influenced by him. In terms of his dramatic style he was far too original to be easily imitated, and he had an unusually creative mind that was continually searching for new techniques of expression. Certainly no twentieth century poet or novelist has experimented so broadly with his art. He was immensely prolific and constantly at work on some literary project Often ideas for new plays would come to him before he had finished the one he was working on. It is likely that future literary historians will see in O'Neill the father of serious dramatic literature in America. Before his plays there is very little worth discussing.

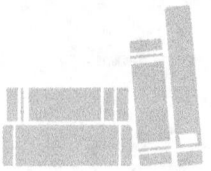

BIBLIOGRAPHY

BOOKS

Alexander, Doris. *The Tempering of Eugene O'Neill*. New York: Hartcourt, Brace and World, Inc., 1962.

[Comprehensive view of O'Neill's early years - ends with the death of James O'Neill, Sr. in 1920.]

Boulton, Agnes. *Part of a Long Story*. Garden City, New York: Doubleday and Company, 1958.

[Mostly chit-chat about the first few years of her marriage to O'Neill.]

Browen, Croswell. *The Curse of the Misbegotten*. New York: McGraw-Hill, 1959.

[Written with the assistance of Shane O'Neill; well-documented and surprisingly unbiased.]

Brown, John Mason. *Dramatis Personae*. New York: Viking Press, 1963.

[Includes this noted reviewer's perceptive commentary and criticism of a number of O'Neill's plays.]

Carpenter, Frederic I. *Eugene O'Neill*. New York: Twayne Publishers, 1964.

[Relates O'Neill's life to his plays - a good quick review of the man and his work.]

Clark, Barrett H. *Eugene O'Neill: The Man and his "Plays."* New York: McBride and Company, 1929.

[One of the earliest books on O'Neill - interesting review of his life and early work.]

Deutsch, Helen and Stella Hanau. *The Provincetown - A Story of the Theatre.* New York: Farrar and Rinehart, 1931.

[An interesting account of the theatre group which greatly influenced O'Neill and vice-versa.]

Dusenbury, Winifred L. *The **Theme** of Loneliness in Modern American Drama.* Gainesville: University of Florida Press, 1960.

[Makes a number of perceptive comments about O'Neill when using his plays to develop her thesis.]

Engel, Edwin. *The Haunted Heroes of Eugene O'Neill.* Cambridge: Harvard University Press, 1953.

[Interesting detailed analysis of major plays and major themes.]

Engel, Edwin A. "Ideas in the Plays of Eugene O'Neill," in *Ideas in the Drama* edited by John Gassner. New York: Columbia University Press, 1964.

[Sees O'Neill's adolescence as the "source of all nourishment and emotional and intellectual."]

Falk, Doris V. *Eugene O'Neill and the Tragic Tension.* Brunswick, New Jersey: Rutgers University Press, 1958.

[Excellent study of O'Neill's plays - many good points and very readable.]

Gagey, Edmond M. "Eugene O'Neill" in *Revolution in American Drama*. New York: Columbia University Press, 1947.

[Brief review of each major play plus a list of O'Neill's important contributions to the theatre.]

Gelb, Arthur and Barbara. *O'Neill*. New York: Harper and Brothers, 1960.

[Most comprehensive work on O'Neill to date - very worthwhile and readable.]

Krutch, Joseph Wood. *The American Drama since 1918*. New York: Random House, 1939.

[Contains an interesting chapter on tragedy which centers on O'Neill.]

Langner, Lawrence. *The Magic Curtain*. New York: E. P. Dutton and Company, 1951.

[This life of Langner contains several chapters on O'Neill and the texts of several of his letters.]

Nathan, George Jean. *The Magic Mirror*. New York: Alfred A. Knopf, 1960.

[Contains several interesting and important essays on O'Neill.]

Parks, Edd Winfield. *Segments of Southern Thought*. Athens: University of Georgia Press, 1938.

[Contains an essay on O'Neill's use of symbolism.]

Quinn, A. H. *A History of the American Drama from the Civil War to the Present Day*. 2. Volumes. New York: Crofts, 1945.

[Interesting section on O'Neill discusses his poetic and mystical qualities.]

Simonson, Lee. *The Stage is Set.* New York: Harcourt, Brace, 1932.

[Many perceptive comments on O'Neill sprinkled throughout the book.]

Skinner, Richard Dana. *Eugene O'Neill: A Poet's Quest.* New York: Longmans, Green and Company, 1935.

[Well-written, perceptive, valuable study of the "inner continuity" of O'Neill's plays.]

Straumann, Heinrich. *American Literature in the Twentieth Century.* London: Hutchinson's University Library, 1951.

[Very brief but very interesting commentary on O'Neill included.]

Winther, Sophus Keith. *Eugene O'Neill: a Critical Study.* New York: Random House, 1934.

[An early study showing considerable insight into the man and his work.]

PERIODICALS

Alexander, Doris M. "Eugene O'Neill as Social Critic," *American Quarterly*, 6 (Winter 1954) 349-363.

[An extended analysis of O'Neill's criticism of modern society.]

Bentley, Eric. "Trying to Like O'Neill," *Kenyon Review*, 14 (July 1952) 476-492.

[A witty, very perceptive article which is widely quoted.]

Brown, John Mason. "Dat Ole Davil and a Hard God," *Saturday Review of Literature*, 35 (February 16, 1952) 32-34.

[Review of *Anna Christie* and *Desire Under the Elms* - contains many interesting comments and comparisons.]

Clark, Barrett H. "Aeschylus and O'Neill," *The English Journal*, XXI, No. 9 (November 1932) 701-705.

[Discusses O'Neill's use of elements of the Greek drama to express problems of modern life.]

Clurman, Harold. "At Odds with Gentility," *Nation*, 194 (April 7, 1962) 312.

[Review of two studies concerning O'Neill - a number of interesting comments.]

De Voto, Bernard. "Minority Report," *Saturday Review*, 15 (November 21, 1936) 3.

[Sharply critical of O'Neill's selection for the Nobel Prize in literature.]

Eaton, Walter Pritchard. "O'Neill: New Risen Attic Stream?" *American Scholar*, 6 (Summer 1937) 304-312.

[Valuable commentary on the Greek tradition as seen in *Desire Under the Elms*.]

Fagin, N. Bryllion. "Eugene O'Neill." *Antioch Review*, 14 (March 1954) 14-26.

[An evaluation of O'Neill published shortly after his death.]

Granger, Bruce J. "Illusion and Reality in Eugene O'Neill," *Modern Language Notes*, 73 (March 1958) 179-186.

[See O'Neill's plays as portraying the dilemma of modern man.]

Hayes, Richard. "Eugene O'Neill: The Tragic in Exile," *Theatre Arts*, 47 (October 1963) 16-17.

[Discussion of O'Neill and his insensibility to words.]

Kemelman, H. G., "Eugene O'Neill and the Highbrow Melodrama," *Bookman*, 75 (September 1932) 482-491.

[A vehement attack on O'Neill and his work which portrays him as a kind of fraud.]

Krutch, Joseph Wood. "Eugene O'Neill, the Lonely Revolutionary," *Theatre Arts*, 36 (April 1952) 29-30.

[Krutch's comments are, as always, pithy and pertinent.]

Krutch, Joseph Wood. "O'Neill's Tragic Sense," *American Scholar*, 16 (Summer 1947) 283-290.

[Discusses difficulty of evaluating O'Neill - concludes he has genius but lacks talent.]

Krutch, Joseph Wood. "Why the O'Neill Star is Rising." *The New York Times Magazine*, (March 19, 1961) 36-37.

[Discusses O'Neill's significance and worth for a new generation.]

Mullett, Mary B. "The Extraordinary Story of Eugene O'Neill," *American Magazine*, 94 (November 1922) 34.

[After forty years, still one of the best portraits of O'Neill ever presented - widely quoted.]

Parks, Edd Winfield. "Eugene O'Neill's Symbolism," *Sewanee Review*, 43 (October-December 1935) 436-450.

[Attempt to explain O'Neill's symbols and philosophy.]

Peck, Seymour. "Talk with Mrs. O'Neill," *New York Times*, 4 (November 1956) 11, 1.6.

[Carlotta Monterey describes the background of *Long Day's Journey* - other interesting comments.]

Stamm, Rudolph. "The Dramatic Experiments of Eugene O'Neill," *English Studies*, 28 (February 1947) 1-15.

[Surveys the main phases of O'Neill's experimentation and development.]

Trilling, Lionel. "Eugene O'Neill," *The New Republic*, 88 (September 23, 1936) 176-179.

[Perceptive discussion of O'Neill's philosophy of life as expressed in his plays.]

Whitman, Robert F. "O'Neill's Search for a Language of the Theatre," *Quarterly Journal of Speech*, XVI, No. 2 (April 1960) 326-332.

[Brief review of O'Neill's many and varied manners of speech: realism, expressionism, symbolism, fantasy, poetry.]

Winther, Sophus Keith. "*Desire Under the Elms*: A Modern Tragedy," *Modern Drama*, 3 (December 1960) 326-332.

[Discussion of the tragedy of modern life in the idiom of ancient Greece.]

Young, Stark. "Eugene O'Neill: Notes from a Critic's Diary." *Harper,* 214 (June 1957) 66-71.

[Interesting, candid article by a personal friend.]

COLLECTIONS OF CRITICAL ARTICLES AND ESSAYS

Cargill, Oscar and others. *O'Neill and His Plays - Four Decades of Criticism.* New York: New York University Press, 1961.

Gassner, John. *O'Neill: A collection of Critical Essays.* Engle wood Cliffs, New Jersey: Prentice-Hall, Inc., 1964.

Miller, Jordan Y. *Playwright's Progress: O'Neill and the Critics.* Fair Lawn, New Jersey: Scott, Foreman and Company, 1965.

www.ingramcontent.com/pod-product-compliance
Lightning Source LLC
LaVergne TN
LVHW011717060526
838200LV00051B/2931